# Multilateral Development Finance 2024

OECD

BETTER POLICIES FOR BETTER LIVES

This work is published under the responsibility of the Secretary-General of the OECD. The opinions expressed and arguments employed herein do not necessarily reflect the official views of the Member countries of the OECD.

This document, as well as any data and map included herein, are without prejudice to the status of or sovereignty over any territory, to the delimitation of international frontiers and boundaries and to the name of any territory, city or area.

**Please cite this publication as:**
OECD (2024), *Multilateral Development Finance 2024*, OECD Publishing, Paris, https://doi.org/10.1787/8f1e2b9b-en.

ISBN 978-92-64-63203-5 (print)
ISBN 978-92-64-96711-3 (PDF)
ISBN 978-92-64-78526-7 (HTML)
ISBN 978-92-64-36953-5 (epub)

Multilateral Development Finance
ISSN 3008-1890 (online)

**Photo credits:** Cover © Fahroni/Shutterstock.com.

Corrigenda to OECD publications may be found at: https://www.oecd.org/en/publications/support/corrigenda.html.

# Foreword

The multilateral development system channels a large and growing share of the official development assistance (ODA) provided by the members of the OECD Development Assistance Committee (DAC), and is asked to address an expanding range of challenges, from poverty reduction and climate change, to pandemics and the impact of Russia's war of aggression against Ukraine. Amid this challenging global context, calls to reform the multilateral system have amplified since 2021, aiming to significantly enhance the system's capacity to deliver on these many fronts.

The *Multilateral Development Finance 2024* report examines the aid flows directed to and from the multilateral development system. It assesses the impact of ongoing reforms, highlighting how members, shareholders and funders can help make it fit for the future. By analysing the state of play in multilateral development finance, the report aims to help DAC members refine their positions in the process leading up to the UN ECOSOC Fourth Financing for Development Conference (FfD4).

Chapter 1 provides an overview of the main findings, including a summary of the recommendations. Chapter 2 discusses the growing relevance of multilateral development finance, and assesses ongoing reform processes that aim to transform the multilateral development system. Chapter 3 explores recent trends in funding to the system (inflows), analysing the funding patterns of DAC members and emerging donors. Chapter 4 sheds light on the activities financed by the multilateral development system (outflows) and highlights the need to carefully maintain the balance between financial capacity and level of concessionality in the context of the growing financialisation of the system.

# Acknowledgements

The Multilateral Development Finance 2024 report was prepared by a team in the OECD Development Co-operation Directorate comprised of Abdoulaye Fabregas, Jieun Kim, Clémence Decisy, Christal Kihm and Gabriele Cristofaro under the overall supervision of Olivier Cattaneo (Head of Unit, Architecture and Analysis). It is part of the directorate's work on multilateral development co-operation.

The report has benefitted from the contributions of many colleagues. The authors would like to particularly thank the following: Erika MacLaughlin and Edward Hainsworth for inputs on multilateral funding structures, collaboration between multilateral organisations, and multilateral development banks' climate action; Ashley Palmer and Valentina Orru, for their contribution on the Global Partnership for Effective Development Co-operation monitoring exercise; Emily Bosch for her contributions on multilateral organisations' pivot to locally-led development; Cushla Thompson, Gregory De Paepe and Cyprien Fabre for their inputs on crisis, conflicts and fragility; Hector Moreno, Giorgio Gualberti, Cécile Sangaré, Aussama Bejraoui, Harsh Desai, Lou Turroques, Sandie Xu and Olivier Bouret for their statistical advice and inputs.

Emily Bosch, Rahul Malhotra, Valentina Orru, Edward Hainsworth, Erika MacLaughlin, Harsh Desai, Cushla Thompson, Gregory De Paepe, Cyprien Fabre, Hector Moreno, Giorgio Gualberti, Cécile Sangaré and Carlotta Schilling have all significantly helped improve the report and the authors are grateful for their review and substantive comments.

The report benefitted from consultations with external partners from research institutes, academia and multilateral organisations, including: the Institute for Sustainable Development and International Relations, German Institute of Development and Sustainability, Dag Hammarskjöld Foundation, University of Glasgow, Center for Global Development, Center for Policy Dialogue, United Nations Development Coordination Office and United Nations Joint Inspection Unit. Members of the OECD Development Assistance Committee (DAC) provided overall strategic guidance.

The authors are grateful for the support received from Stephanie Coic on graphic design, as well as for the editorial support provided by Fiona Hinchcliffe. Joelle Bassoul, Ola Kasneci, Karena Garnier, Meria Greco and Jessica Voorhees facilitated the publication and communications process, and Henri-Bernard Solignac-Lecomte provided strategic communications advice.

# Table of contents

Foreword 3

Acknowledgements 4

Abbreviations and acronyms 8

Executive summary 10

1 Overview 13

High stakes amid high risks: reforming multilateral development co-operation in a changing world 13
Funding to the multilateral development system (inflows) 16
Financing from the multilateral development system (outflows) 22
Towards a future-fit multilateral development system 25
References 29
Notes 30

2 High stakes amid high risks: reforming multilateral development co-operation in a changing world 31

Multilateral finance is increasingly central in the development co-operation landscape 32
New global challenges call for multilateral development finance to expand its focus and capabilities 38
A coherent and well-balanced architecture is crucial for successful multilateral reform 44
Key chapter findings and recommendations 50
References 52
Notes 54

3 Funding to the multilateral development system 55

The crisis-induced growth of multilateral development finance is exacerbating existing tensions in the system 56
DAC members play a vital role through their support to and engagement with the multilateral development system 66
Emerging donors are slowly reshaping multilateral institutions' funding base 73
Key chapter findings and solutions 82
References 84

4 Financing from the multilateral system 86
Financing from the multilateral development system is resilient amidst multiple shocks and crises 87
The system is venturing beyond traditional mandates to tackle cutting-edge development challenges 91
Multilateral organisations are torn between their traditional roles and new mandates and responsibilities 103
Overview of key chapter findings and solutions 108
References 110
Notes 112

## FIGURES

Figure 1.1. The shares of funding to (inflows) and financing by (outflows) the multilateral development system are both steadily increasing 14
Figure 1.2. The planned increase in MDB lending capacity will fall short of expectations 15
Figure 1.3. In 2022, a sharp rise in earmarking contrasted with a decline in core multilateral contributions 17
Figure 1.4. The rise of earmarking is no longer specific to the UN 18
Figure 1.5. Multilateral contributions would have stagnated without earmarked crisis response funding 18
Figure 1.6. While funding to the UNDS is rising steadily, MDBs increasingly rely on financial innovation 20
Figure 1.7. China, the UAE, and India are among the largest and fastest-growing donors to the UNDS 21
Figure 1.8. Multilateral outflows have rebounded and are close to reaching 2020's peak levels 22
Figure 1.9. Multilateral organisations adjust their sectoral allocations to tackle successive crises 23
Figure 1.10. Multilateral organisations are able to focus on poverty through concessional finance 24
Figure 1.11. Many multilateral organisations that increase financing tend to reduce the share of concessional finance 25
Figure 1.12. Three deep currents – of expansion, diversification and fragmentation – are gradually changing the face of multilateral development finance 26
Figure 2.1. Multilateral organisations are an essential link in the development assistance chain 32
Figure 2.2. The "market share" of the multilateral development system has grown by 36% over the past ten years 33
Figure 2.3. The long-run trend shows a slow but steady increase in the use of the multilateral system 35
Figure 2.4. All DAC countries that meet the 0.7% of ODA/GNI target make significant use of the multilateral system 36
Figure 2.5. Lending from multilateral creditors was not sufficient to counterbalance negative private capital outflows in 2022 38
Figure 2.6. The multilateral development system is continuously evolving 39
Figure 2.7. The current MDB reform drive could support a 30% increase in MDB financing 41
Figure 2.8. The estimates of additional lending capacity from the MDB reform remains far from initial expectations 42
Figure 2.9. The multilateral architecture is comprised of a growing number of entities 44
Figure 2.10. The number of multilateral donors in ODA-eligible countries has increased substantially over the past decade 46
Figure 2.11. The average project size in vertical funds and UN entities has decreased 48
Figure 3.1. In 2022, a sharp rise in earmarking contrasted with a decline in core multilateral contributions 56
Figure 3.2. Recent crises have accelerated the use of earmarked contributions 57
Figure 3.3. The rise of earmarking is no longer specific to the UN 58
Figure 3.4. Without crisis-response earmarking, multilateral contributions would have stagnated 60
Figure 3.5. Humanitarian aid does not drive the recent peak in earmarked contributions 62
Figure 3.6. Funding to the UNDS is rising while MDBs need to innovate to compensate for flat donor contributions 63
Figure 3.7. The creation of new funds adds layers of complexity to the multilateral architecture 64
Figure 3.8. The concessional windows of the legacy MDBs compete for resources with the vertical funds created over the past two decades 66
Figure 3.9. The United States, Germany and France accounted for half of DAC members' contributions to the multilateral development system in 2022 67

Figure 3.10. More than 80% of DAC members have increased their multilateral contributions since 2019, although levels vary 68
Figure 3.11. The largest DAC providers do not necessarily contribute their "fair share" of funding to the multilateral development system 69
Figure 3.12. The multilateral system is being used more but invested in less 71
Figure 3.13. Even historic core supporters reduced their share of core contributions 72
Figure 3.14. As a group, emerging donors are the 8th largest UNDS' government contributor 74
Figure 3.15. China, the UAE, and India are amongst the largest and fastest-growing donors to the UNDS 75
Figure 3.16. China and Saudi Arabia are amongst the largest and fastest-growing donors to IDA replenishments 76
Figure 3.17. Emerging donors and DAC members have different funding patterns 77
Figure 3.18. Among emerging donors, only Saudi Arabia and the UAE make greater use of earmarked than core contributions to the UNDS 78
Figure 3.19. Emerging donors and DAC members differ in their contributions to UN entities and shares to the UN Secretariat 79
Figure 3.20. Emerging donors' shareholdings vary significantly across the legacy MDBs 80
Figure 3.21. Emerging donors are the largest shareholders in the newer, Southern-led MDBs 81
Figure 4.1. Multilateral outflows in 2022 recovered from the previous year's temporary decline 87
Figure 4.2. Outflows from the World Bank Group and other MDBs have increased most since 2012 88
Figure 4.3. Multilateral organisations can adjust their sectoral allocations to respond to crises 89
Figure 4.4. Vertical funds allow the multilateral development system to pivot between crises 90
Figure 4.5. Social sectors have benefitted differently from recent crises 91
Figure 4.6. Multilateral organisations have driven the increase in private finance mobilisation 92
Figure 4.7. Multilateral organisations use a diverse range of instruments to mobilise private finance 94
Figure 4.8. Only a small amount of private finance is mobilised in least developed countries 96
Figure 4.9. Among the green funds, only the Green Climate Fund approaches MDBs' financial capacity 98
Figure 4.10. MDBs' climate-related development finance has increased and adaptation represents a growing share 99
Figure 4.11. MDBs' climate finance mainly targets mitigation-relevant sectors despite an increase in the share of adaptation finance 101
Figure 4.12. Multilateral organisations are able to focus on poverty through their concessional finance 104
Figure 4.13. Multilateral organisations prioritise social sectors more than bilateral donors 105
Figure 4.14. An increasing share of earmarked funds are unallocated, meaning less funds for low-income countries 106
Figure 4.15. Earmarked and core multilateral flows increasingly target global public goods 106
Figure 4.16. Different types of multilateral organisations vary in their poverty and inequality focus 107
Figure 4.17. Many multilateral organisations are increasing financing while reducing the share of concessional finance 108

## TABLES

Table 2.1. There are large differences in implementation rate across MDBs and MDB reform areas 43
Table 3.1. Replenishments in the multilateral development system rely on a few major official providers 65
Table 3.2. DAC members can help multilateral actors shift to locally led development 70

# Abbreviations and acronyms

| | |
|---|---|
| ADB | Asian Development Bank |
| AfDB | African Development Bank |
| AIIB | Asian Infrastructure Investment Bank |
| CRS | Creditor Reporting System |
| DAC | Development Assistance Committee |
| EBRD | European Bank for Reconstruction and Development |
| EIB | European Investment Bank |
| GCF | Green Climate Fund |
| GPEDC | Global Partnership for Effective Development Co-operation |
| GPG | Global public good |
| IADB | Inter-American Development Bank |
| IBRD | International Bank for Reconstruction and Development |
| IDA | International Development Association |
| IEG | G20 Independent Expert Group |
| IFC | International Finance Corporation |
| IFIs | International financial institutions |
| IMF | International Monetary Fund |
| IsDB | Islamic Development Bank |
| LDC | Least developed country |
| LIC | Low-income country |
| LMIC | Lower-middle income country |
| MDB | Multilateral development bank |
| MIGA | Multilateral Investment Guarantee Agency |
| MOPAN | Multilateral Organisation Performance Assessment Network |
| NDB | New Development Bank |
| OECD | Organisation for Economic Co-operation and Development |
| ODA | Official development assistance |

| | |
|---|---|
| ODF | Official development finance |
| OOF | Other official flows |
| RDB | Regional Development Bank |
| SPV | Special purpose vehicle |
| UMIC | Upper-middle income country |
| UNDS | United Nations Development System |
| UNRWA | United Nations Relief and Works Agency for Palestine Refugees in the Near East |
| USD | United States dollar |
| WBG | World Bank Group |
| WHO | World Health Organization |

# Executive summary

The multilateral system is a significant and growing player in development co-operation. Encompassing more than 200 organisations – including those within the United Nations Development System (UNDS), as well as multilateral development banks (MDBs) and vertical funds – today the system delivers nearly two-thirds of all official development finance. This report, the fourth edition since 2018, presents the state of play in multilateral development finance, highlighting key trends and their implications, and making recommendations for sustaining its development impact in increasingly challenging times.

## The risk of financialisation: losing sight of development goals

The growing array of development challenges – from poverty reduction to climate change, and the impact of Russia's war of aggression against Ukraine – is accentuating the pressure on the multilateral development system to evolve more quickly. The current reform drive, largely focused on strengthening the system's financing capacity, is placing hefty expectations on the MDBs, pushing them to do more with the same or fewer resources. These institutions are urged to rely on financial innovation, extending a decade-long trend of "financialisation" which has seen them increasingly leverage their balance sheets to offset stagnating donor contributions. As a result, outflows from the World Bank Group and other MDBs rose substantially between 2012 and 2020, by 72% in the case of the World Bank Group (USD 35.3 billion) and by 155% for other MDBs (USD 61.8 billion).

Yet, relying on financial innovation will not be sufficient to meet expanded multilateral mandates, including tackling climate change, while maintaining support for traditional and vital areas such as poverty reduction. While MDBs have taken steps to grow their lending capacity, analysis in this report finds that these measures could at best allow for a 30% increase by 2030 – far short of the G20 Independent Expert Group's call for tripling MDB lending capacity by that date.

The financialisation process behind the expansion of the multilateral development system's financing capacities has seen a rise in non-concessional lending. This is particularly concerning amid heightened debt risks in developing countries: concessional finance must be preserved to ensure the continuity of multilateral support in challenging contexts, and fight poverty, which remains central to multilateral organisations' mandates. Financial innovation must be balanced with additional donor contributions to manage the trade-off between scaling up overall financing and ensuring that concessional resources are available for the poorest and most vulnerable countries.

## Investing in the system to deliver on expanded multilateral mandates

The expansion of the system raises other threats. Multilateral growth has contributed to an increasingly complex and crowded architecture, leading to fragmentation and presenting significant challenges to division of labour, co-ordination and overall effectiveness. Despite ambitious calls to strengthen the multilateral development system, the recent funding increases have predominantly come from contributions earmarked for crisis response, while the share of core funding for long-term development has fallen. Thus, although OECD DAC members are channelling more aid through the multilateral system than ever before, they appear less inclined to invest in its core, strategic functions, as evidenced by the 6% decline in core contributions registered in 2022. Although the system's ability to pivot swiftly between crises is important, it should not detract from the need to invest in the system through core contributions, which ensure that multilateral organisations can maintain a focus on key long-term sustainable development goals, such as poverty and climate.

## Balancing efficiency with effectiveness: an agenda for multilateral fitness

The current reform momentum offers a rare opportunity to strengthen the multilateral development system and equip it to achieve the global development agenda. However, there is a risk that reforms will fail if they remain narrowly focused on increasing financial efficiency.

DAC members, as the main shareholders and funders of the multilateral development system, can help support a well-balanced and effectively governed multilateral development system. This requires complementing efficiency (doing more with existing resources) with effectiveness (allocating more and better resources to deliver on mandates while ensuring transparency and accountability) and adopting a system-wide perspective (reforming other parts of the system beyond MDBs and promoting greater co-ordination and coherence).

## Outlining solutions for a future-fit multilateral development system

Building on the analysis, the report makes recommendations organised around the three dimensions of multilateral development finance outlined in its three main chapters:

1. **Multilateral architecture and reform processes**

- Prioritise the rationalisation of the multilateral architecture in global discussions, such as the Fourth Financing for Development (FfD4) Conference and G20 meetings.
- Promote greater collaboration in multilateral reforms, using existing fora to share experiences and lessons from organisations engaged in reform processes.
- Strengthen dialogue in capitals among aid agencies, ministries of foreign affairs and treasuries on cross-cutting issues such as MDB reform, to balance financial and development considerations.
- Address the lack of standardisation in bilateral and multilateral donors' reporting requirements to reduce the burden on multilateral organisations and recipient countries.
- Reinvigorate the dialogue between multilateral and bilateral providers on the aid effectiveness principles and accelerate and monitor their implementation in multilateral development co-operation.

2. **Funding to the multilateral system (inflows)**

- Ensure successful replenishments of MDB concessional windows and global funds, and additional capital contributions, capitalising on their multiplier effect.
- Secure adequate funding for core strategic functions, including by increasing the level of core contributions to rebalance core and earmarked contributions to UN organisations.
- Prioritise flexible funding, such as contributions to multi-donor and inter-agency pooled funds, which foster co-ordination and enable organisations to adapt to countries' needs.
- Engage with emerging donors on multilateral development finance, using existing OECD DAC outreach mechanisms, such as regional policy dialogues, to develop common ground for good practices.

**3. Financing from the multilateral system (outflows)**

- Safeguard the system's capacity to support the poorest and most vulnerable. Assess the allocative impact of multilateral organisations' reforms and increase their concessional resources.
- Promote greater complementarity of multilateral aid portfolios by supporting research on multilateral aid portfolios to inform reforms and programming.
- Support a greater role for multilateral organisations in creating a conducive environment for private investment at the country level to complement the current focus on deploying financial instruments at the project level.
- Accelerate climate action, strengthening efforts to expand adaptation finance, including by mainstreaming climate into sectors beyond infrastructure and production.

# 1 Overview

This report presents the state of play in multilateral development finance, highlighting key trends and their implications. It examines recent and ongoing developments in multilateral development finance through the lenses of (1) the multilateral architecture and reforms; (2) funding to the multilateral system (inflows); and (3) financing from the multilateral system (outflows). The analysis sheds light on various shifts and challenges affecting the system, and feeds into policy recommendations, summarised at the end of this overview.

## High stakes amid high risks: reforming multilateral development co-operation in a changing world

### *Multilateral finance occupies an increasingly central place in development co-operation*

**In an era of overlapping crises and development challenges, the multilateral system channels a large and growing share of official development assistance (ODA).** The system encompasses more than 200 organisations mandated by their members and shareholders to promote international development. These include entities within the United Nations Development System (UNDS), multilateral development banks (MDBs) and vertical funds. OECD Development Assistance Committee (DAC) members' contributions to multilateral organisations, representing inflows to the system, have steadily increased over the past decade. From 37% in 2010, the share of DAC members' funding channelled to or through multilateral organisations rose to 45% in 2021, before slightly declining to 43% in 2022 (Figure 1.1, Panel A.). This overall upward trend in multilateral inflows reflects donors' recognition of the multilateral system's value in delivering aid projects to support sustainable development (OECD, 2020[1]).

**Nearly two-thirds of official development finance is delivered by multilateral organisations.** Multilateral organisations' extensive reach, technical expertise and capacity make them indispensable for orchestrating collective responses to global development challenges (OECD, 2020[1]). As a result, through their outflows multilateral organisations deliver a large and growing share of total official development finance (ODF) to ODA-eligible countries. Between 2012 and 2022, the multilateral development system's share of total ODF reached 61% (Figure 1.1, Panel B), up from 45% in 2012. This growth was driven both by the increase in donor contributions and by some multilateral organisations' ability to leverage their resources by tapping into the capital markets.

### Figure 1.1. The shares of funding to (inflows) and financing by (outflows) the multilateral development system are both steadily increasing

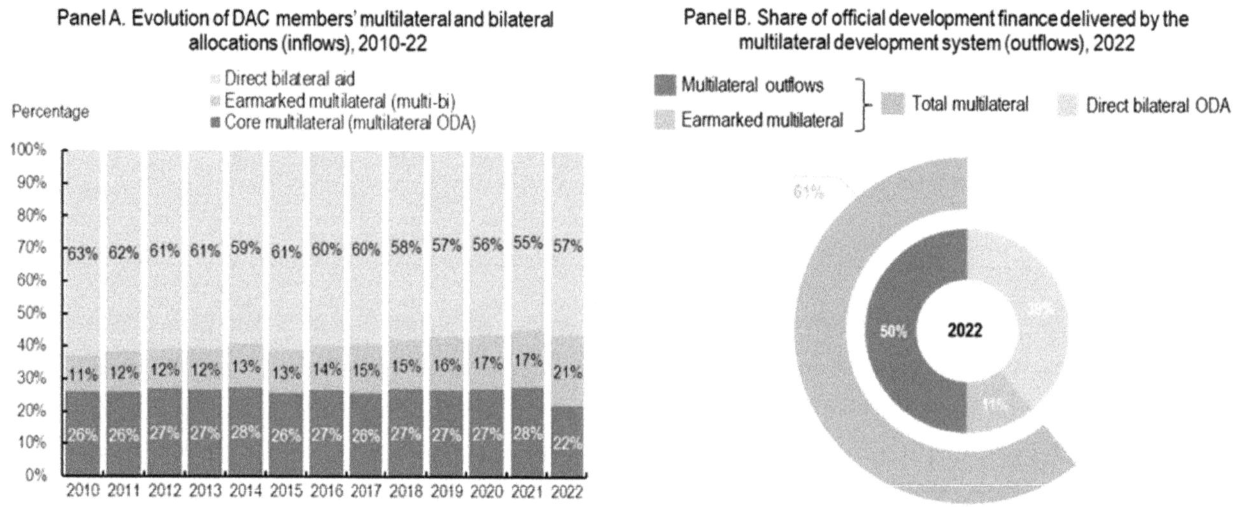


Note: Direct bilateral ODA refers to DAC members' bilateral ODA excluding multi-bi aid (non-core contributions to multilateral organisations). Calculations are based on gross disbursements in 2022 constant prices.
Source: Authors' calculations based on OECD (2024[2]), OECD Data Explorer, DAC1 Table, http://data-explorer.oecd.org/s/t for Panel A and OECD (2024[3]), OECD Data Explorer, *Creditor Reporting System* (database), http://data-explorer.oecd.org/s/c for Panel B.

StatLink https://stat.link/krt2yz

### *The multilateral development system is at the forefront of the global financial architecture reform*

**Faced with a growing array of development challenges, the multilateral development system is under pressure to accelerate its evolution.** The widening gap between countries' aspirations and their financial resources has sparked calls to reform the global financial architecture. Recent calls for reform have drawn attention to the financial limitations of the current system and the need to scale up multilateral development finance to ensure the system is equipped to fulfil expanded mandates in a context of multiple overlapping crises. Specifically, these calls for reform underscore the need to expand the scope of intervention and capacity of the major international financial institutions (IFIs), particularly the main MDBs and the International Monetary Fund (US Department of State, 2022[4]; Government of Barbados, 2022[5]).

**As part of the current reform drive, the main IFIs have been asked by their shareholders and members to undergo a triple transformation.** This involves: (1) expanding their mandates beyond their traditional focus on poverty and inequality to also address global challenges, including support to global public goods (GPGs) such as climate change; (2) improving how these institutions operate, including by transforming their country engagement, to ensure they deliver enhanced development outcomes; and (3) transforming the multilateral toolbox by leveraging financial innovation to increase MDBs' lending capacity and accelerate the mobilisation of private finance.

**However, the financial gains from current multilateral reforms – though significant – risk falling short of initial expectations.** At the 2024 World Bank-IMF Spring meetings, ten MDBs[1] estimated that they could collectively expand their lending headroom by an additional USD 300 billion to USD 400 billion over the coming ten years (African Development Bank et al., 2024[6]). This would represent a 30% increase on their pre-COVID-19 commitment levels. Even under this optimistic scenario, this equates to just USD 40 billion more per year – substantially less than the additional USD 260 billion per year called for by the G20 Independent Expert Group (IEG) to meet the Sustainable Development Goals. By 2030, this discrepancy could amount to a cumulative financing shortfall of around USD 755 billion (Figure 1.2). Bridging this substantial gap would require exploring new options – including additional donor contributions – beyond the balance sheet optimisation measures and financial innovations currently under consideration.

**The current reform focus on the MDBs should not distract from the need to strengthen the other parts of the multilateral development system or to complete unfinished reforms.** The current reform momentum offers a rare opportunity to strengthen the multilateral development system and equip it to achieve the global development agenda. However, there is a risk the reforms will fail to deliver if efforts remain narrowly focused on increasing the financial efficiency of the MDBs. A well-balanced and effectively governed multilateral development system requires complementing efficiency (doing more with existing resources) with effectiveness (allocating more and better resources to deliver on mandates while ensuring transparency and accountability) and adopting a system-wide perspective (reforming other parts of the system beyond MDBs and promoting greater co-ordination). This will involve tackling unfinished reform processes in other parts of the system, such as the recently updated UN Funding Compact (United Nations, 2024[7]), and addressing often-neglected reform areas, such as funding quality and coherence of the multilateral architecture. These factors are gaining importance as the system's constant growth introduces vulnerabilities that need to be balanced with structural and systemic improvements.

## Figure 1.2. The planned increase in MDB lending capacity will fall short of expectations

MDB commitments (2006-22) and pathways for scaling up MDB financing capacity (2022-32)

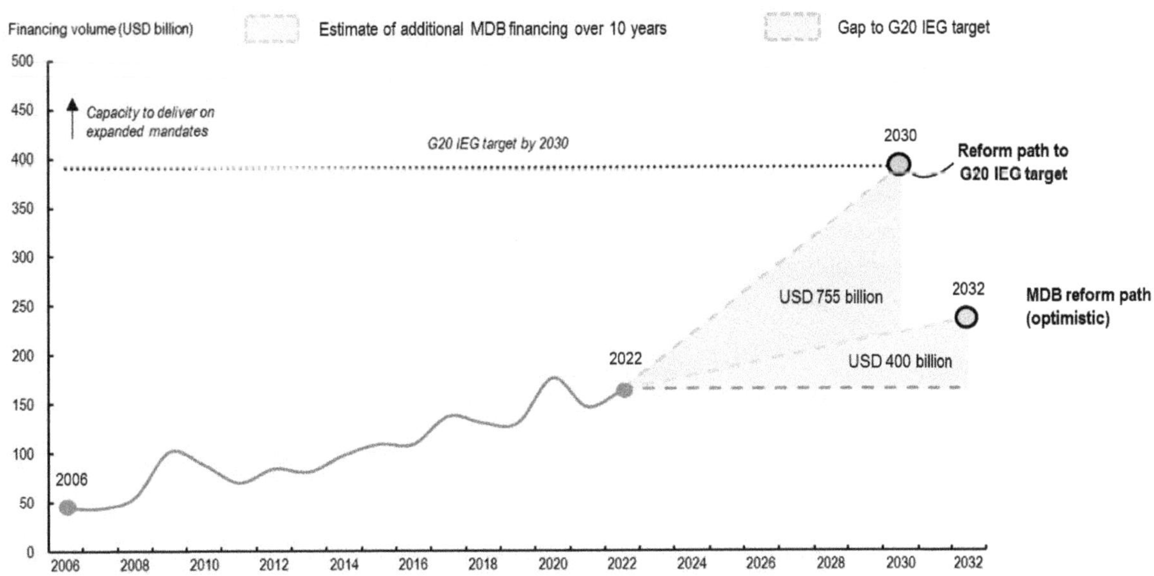


Source: Authors' calculations based on OECD (2024[3]), OECD Data Explorer, *Creditor Reporting System* (database), https://stats.oecd.org/Index.aspx?DataSetCode=crs1; and African Development Bank et al. (2024[6]), *MDBs Working as a System for Impact and Scale*, https://www.iadb.org/document.cfm?id=EZIDB0000577-986313001-135.

StatLink https://stat.link/1lboas

### *Multilateral growth has contributed to an increasingly complex architecture*

**The growth of multilateral development finance in response to new development challenges has been accompanied by an expansion of the multilateral architecture.** Stakeholders of the multilateral development system tend to establish new entities in response to each new crisis or development challenge: the number of entities on the list of ODA-eligible international organisations rose from 121 in 2000 to 212 in 2020. As new organisations are created and existing ones broaden their mandates and operational capabilities, the multilateral development architecture becomes more versatile, but also more intricate.

**The continued expansion of the multilateral development system leads to fragmentation.** Over time, a crowded and complex architecture can present significant challenges in terms of division of labour, co-ordination and overall effectiveness. At the country level, the presence of a growing number of multilateral providers can complicate co-ordination and undermine country ownership. Some multilateral organisations are stretching their resources across an increasing number of activities, sectors and recipients. This not only complicates the management and oversight of projects – it also reduces the potential for achieving substantial, transformative outcomes in recipient countries.

## Funding to the multilateral development system (inflows)

### *The crisis-induced growth in multilateral contributions exacerbates existing tensions in the system*

**Although there is a variety of multilateral organisations with different funding models, members and shareholders represent a vital source of funding.** Their contributions to the multilateral development system can be divided into two types. The first are core contributions, also referred to as multilateral ODA, which consist of funding that multilateral organisations can allocate as they see fit, within the parameters set by their governing board. The second are earmarked contributions, also known as non-core or multi-bi aid, which are funds targeted to specific sectors, themes, countries or regions. The sum of core and non-core contributions constitutes official providers' total use of the multilateral system. This combined total offers a more comprehensive indication of how donors use the multilateral development system since it takes into account all types of funding provided to, or channelled through, multilateral organisations.

**In 2022, DAC members' total use of the multilateral system reached a new record high, totalling USD 98.5 billion.** This marks the seventh consecutive annual increase in total use of the multilateral system. This amount comprised USD 50.6 billion in core contributions (multilateral ODA), while earmarked contributions (non-core or multi-bi aid) amounted to USD 48 billion (Figure 1.3, Panel A).

**Figure 1.3. In 2022, a sharp rise in earmarking contrasted with a decline in core multilateral contributions**

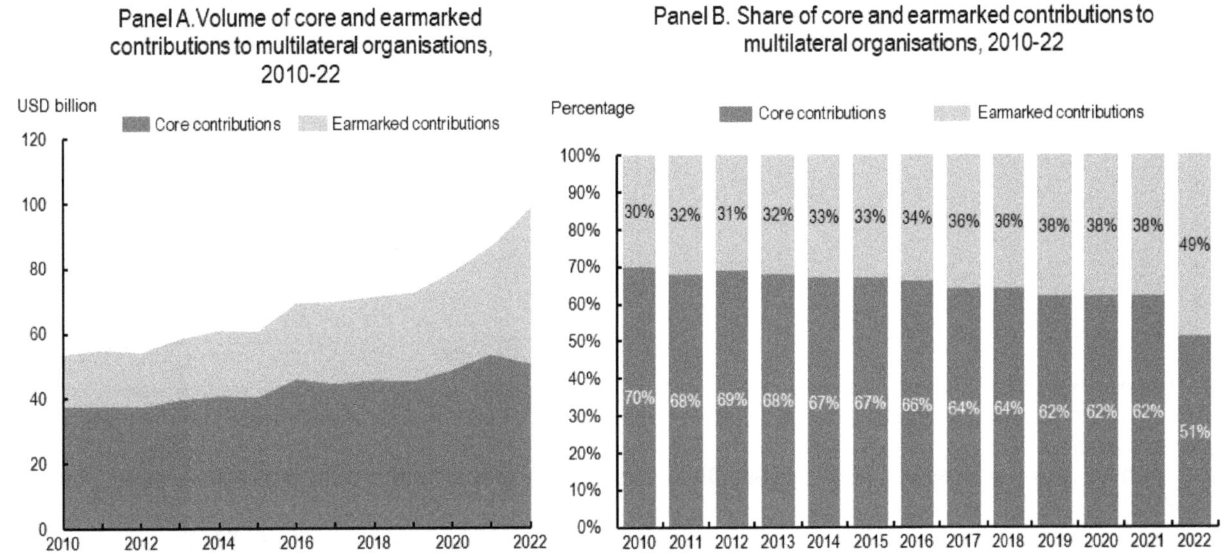


Note: The two graphs present DAC countries' total use of the multilateral development system, which covers both their core contributions (multilateral ODA) and their earmarked contributions (non-core, or multi-bi aid) to multilateral organisations. Calculations are based on disbursements, in 2022 constant prices.
Source: Authors' calculations based on OECD (2024[8]), OECD Data Explorer, "Members' total use of the multilateral system", http://data-explorer.oecd.org/s/s.

StatLink https://stat.link/filjh2

**Exceptional levels of support to Ukraine through earmarked contributions largely drove the 2022 increase in the total use of the multilateral development system.** Several DAC members provided significant support to Ukraine, primarily as budget support through the MDBs. Overall, while earmarked contributions surged by 42% between 2021 and 2022, however, core contributions dipped by 6%. This led to a significant rise in the share of earmarked contributions as a percentage of total contributions observed in 2022. Over the past decade, earmarked contributions have gradually but steadily increased from 30% in 2010 to 38% in 2021. Between 2021 and 2022, however, this share surged by 11 percentage points, from 38% to 49% (Figure 1.3, Panel B).

**Earmarked contributions, already entrenched in the UNDS, are becoming more apparent across the rest of the multilateral development system.** Previous editions of the report have shown that reliance on earmarked contributions varies across multilateral organisations, with the practice of earmarking being particularly prevalent within the UNDS (OECD, 2015[9]). Successive crises in recent years have led to a widespread increase in earmarking across the entire multilateral development system. Figure 1.4 depicts how earmarked contributions to the World Bank Group rapidly rose in 2022, in large part as a means to channel finance to Ukraine. Earmarking to the IMF also surged, as donors channelled funds through the Poverty Reduction and Growth Trust (PRGT), likely with the aim to support countries affected by successive crises.

## Figure 1.4. The rise of earmarking is no longer specific to the UN

DAC countries' core and earmarked contributions to multilateral organisations, 2010-22

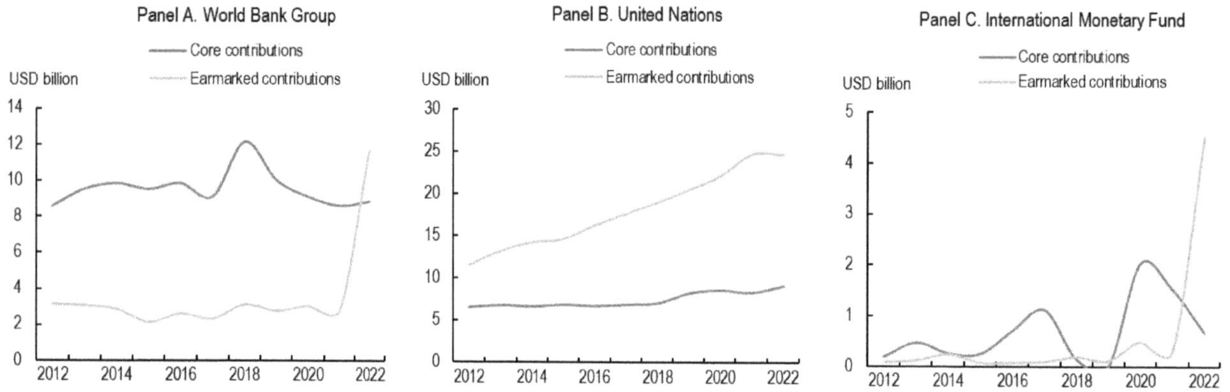


Note: The graphs present DAC countries' total use of the multilateral development system, which covers both their core contributions (multilateral ODA) and their earmarked contributions (non-core, or multi-bi aid) to multilateral organisations. Calculations are based on gross disbursements, in 2022 constant prices.

Source: Authors' calculations based on OECD (2024[8]), OECD Data Explorer, *Members' total use of the multilateral system* (database), http://data-explorer.oecd.org/s/s.

StatLink https://stat.link/bgu9w6

**The growth in multilateral contributions is driven by crisis response, rather than long-term sustainable development priorities.** When excluding funds earmarked for recent crises, contributions to the multilateral development system remained relatively flat between 2012 and 2022 (Figure 1.5). In fact, multilateral contributions would have stagnated if not for the funding earmarked for crisis response. Notably, contributions earmarked for humanitarian assistance, the response to the COVID-19 pandemic and Ukraine rose by more than 400% over the ten-year period, compared to a more limited 43% increase in other multilateral contributions.

## Figure 1.5. Multilateral contributions would have stagnated without earmarked crisis response funding

DAC countries' core contributions and earmarked contributions for humanitarian, COVID-19, Ukraine and other development purposes, 2012-22

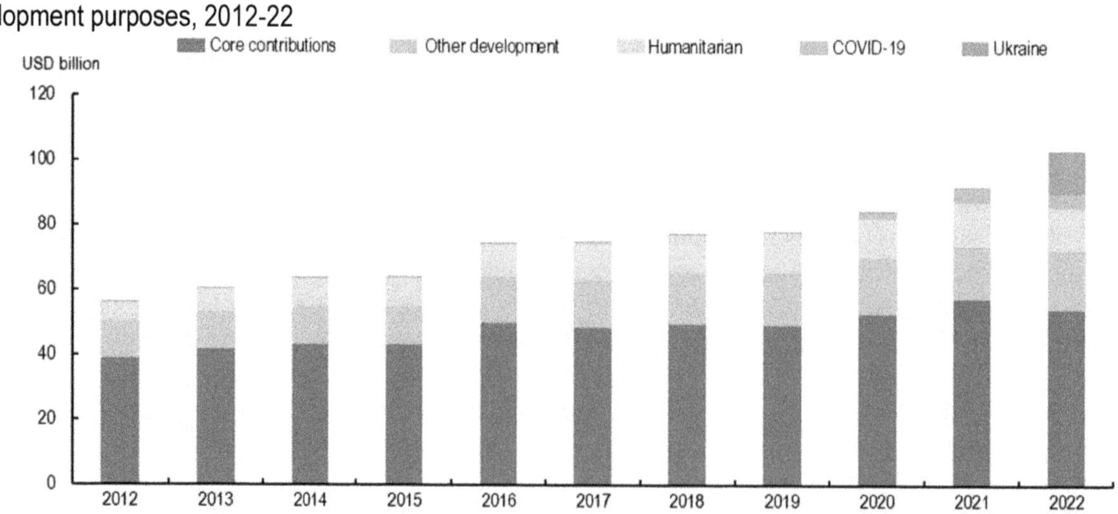


Note: Calculations are based on DAC countries' gross disbursements, in 2022 constant prices. Contributions earmarked for humanitarian aid correspond to those reported to the Creditor Reporting System under sector codes 720, 730 and 740. Contributions earmarked for COVID-19 correspond to those reported under the purpose code 12264. Contributions earmarked for Ukraine are those reported under the recipient code 85.

Source: Authors' calculations based on OECD (2024[8]), OECD Data Explorer, *Members' total use of the multilateral system* (database), http://data-explorer.oecd.org/s/s.

StatLink https://stat.link/icv9aq

**To deliver on the global sustainable development agenda, multilateral organisations need resources that enable them to tackle long-term development challenges.** While the multilateral development system's ability to pivot swiftly between crises is an important feature, maintaining a focus on other key sustainable development goals requiring a long-term horizon, such as poverty reduction and climate, is equally important. The recent rise of earmarked contributions for crisis response should not detract from the need to invest in the system through core contributions, which ensure that multilateral organisations can help developing countries achieve vital long-term objectives. These core resources are essential as they provide multilateral organisations with the flexibility to allocate funding according to the evolving needs of recipient countries. Moreover, a strong base of core funding helps safeguard the financial health and operational integrity of multilateral institutions by providing the financial foundation for their corporate functions, such as human resources management, strategic planning, and monitoring and evaluation. Ultimately, a continued shift towards earmarked funding can undermine the capacity of these institutions to pursue their core mandates effectively and sustainably.

**Maintaining a critical mass of core contributions thus remains essential for ensuring the system's ability to respond to global development challenges**. Some organisations, such as the World Health Organization (WHO), are making efforts to rebalance the share of core versus earmarked contributions. These demonstrate that though challenging, rebalancing funding models to reduce over-reliance on earmarked contributions is feasible with concerted effort and commitment from all multilateral stakeholders.

### *Stagnating donor contributions to the MDBs are driving the financialisation of the system*

**Funding to UN entities and vertical funds saw a sharp increase, driven by the need to address recent crises.** The traditional funding model of these institutions, which largely relies on members' contributions, led to a substantial increase in funding to address the additional needs generated by these crises. For instance, funding to the UNDS more than doubled between 2012 and 2022, rising from USD 19.0 billion to USD 41.9 billion (Figure 1.6).

**By contrast, contributions to the MDBs have remained relatively flat over the past decade, reflecting their growing reliance on financial innovation.** This trend of flat or declining contributions stands in stark contrast to the MDBs' growing outflows over the same period. This divergence is driving MDBs' increasing reliance on financial innovation to boost their financing capacity. Such innovation includes efforts to increase MDB lending through balance sheet optimisation measures such as merging their concessional and non-concessional windows and risk transfer agreements (OECD, 2022[10]). Since 2021, this has been reinforced by the reforms that are demanding these institutions do more with the same or even fewer resources by relying even further on balance sheet optimisation and the use of innovative financial instruments, such as donor guarantees and hybrid capital instruments.[2] Ultimately, these trends result in a financialisation of the system, characterised by a growing dependence of development finance providers on financial instruments, financial markets, financial motives and financial institutions for managing and implementing development co-operation activities.

**Figure 1.6. While funding to the UNDS is rising steadily, MDBs increasingly rely on financial innovation**

DAC members' contributions by category of multilateral organisation, 2012-22

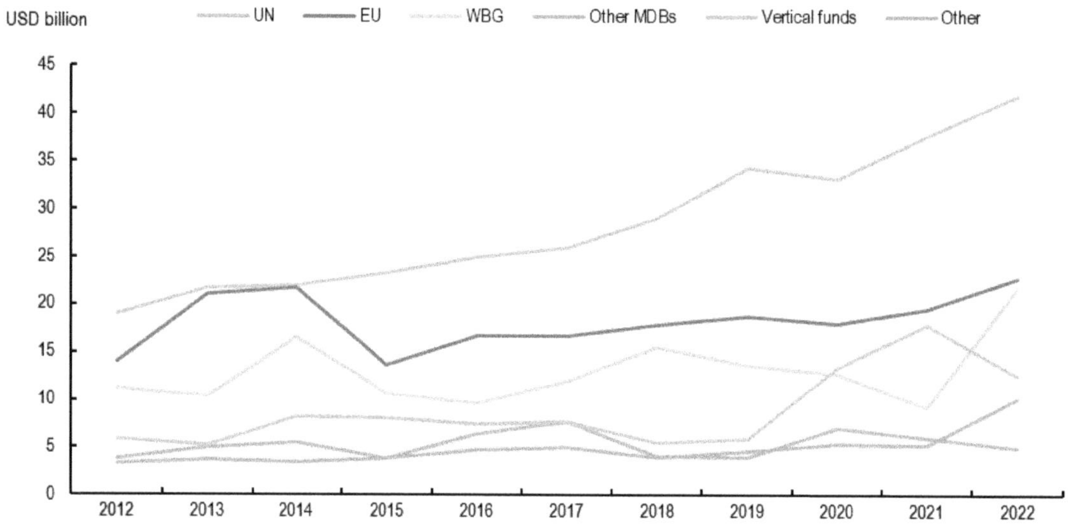


Note: Calculations are based on DAC countries' gross disbursements, in 2022 constant prices. Contributions include both core and earmarked funding.
Source: Authors' calculations based on (OECD, 2024[8]), OECD Data Explorer, *Members' total use of the multilateral system* (database), http://data-explorer.oecd.org/s/s.

StatLink https://stat.link/lu1j6t

**Although the financialisation of the multilateral development system has been beneficial for increasing MDB financing capacity, it will not be sufficient to achieve MDB reform targets.** Financial innovations are essential for leveraging additional resources, but they should not overshadow the critical need for consistent and substantial donor contributions that capitalise on the multiplier effect of MDBs' leverage capacity. For example, for every dollar contributed by donors, the World Bank Group's concessional arm, IDA, can provide four dollars for sustainable development (World Bank Group, 2024[11]). Similarly, general capital increases for major MDBs can unlock additional financing capacity that far outweigh the contributions of donors. For instance, the USD 13 billion in paid-in capital provided by the World Bank Group's shareholders during the institution's latest general capital increase in 2018 boosted its lending capacity by about USD 41 billion annually through 2030 (Kenny and Morris, 2021[12]). Conversely, for donors, not capitalising on such high-impact funding modalities, and instead prioritising unleveraged contributions through trust funds, represents a significant opportunity cost.

### *Emerging donors are slowly reshaping the funding base of multilateral institutions*

**Although DAC members continue to play a pivotal role in the multilateral development system, a few emerging donors are progressively assuming greater prominence**. DAC countries remain the largest funders of the multilateral development system. Collectively, they accounted for 95% of donor contributions to the UNDS in 2022, while emerging donors contributed approximately 4% and other official donors made up the remaining 1%. However, a few emerging actors are gradually carving out a leadership role in the multilateral development system. Specifically, the People's Republic of China became the 15th largest donor to the UN Development System in 2022, a significant leap from 23rd in 2012 (Figure 1.7). Moreover, the country boosted its contributions to IDA replenishments by 763% between IDA16 and IDA20 (completed in 2010 and 2022). This placed China among the top 20 largest contributors to IDA20, alongside Saudi Arabia and India. India's rise is particularly remarkable, as the country did not contribute to IDA16 in 2010 but has become one of the largest IDA contributors in 2022.

### Figure 1.7. China, the UAE, and India are among the largest and fastest-growing donors to the UNDS

Funding to UNDS, 2022, and % change in contributions, 2012 versus 2022

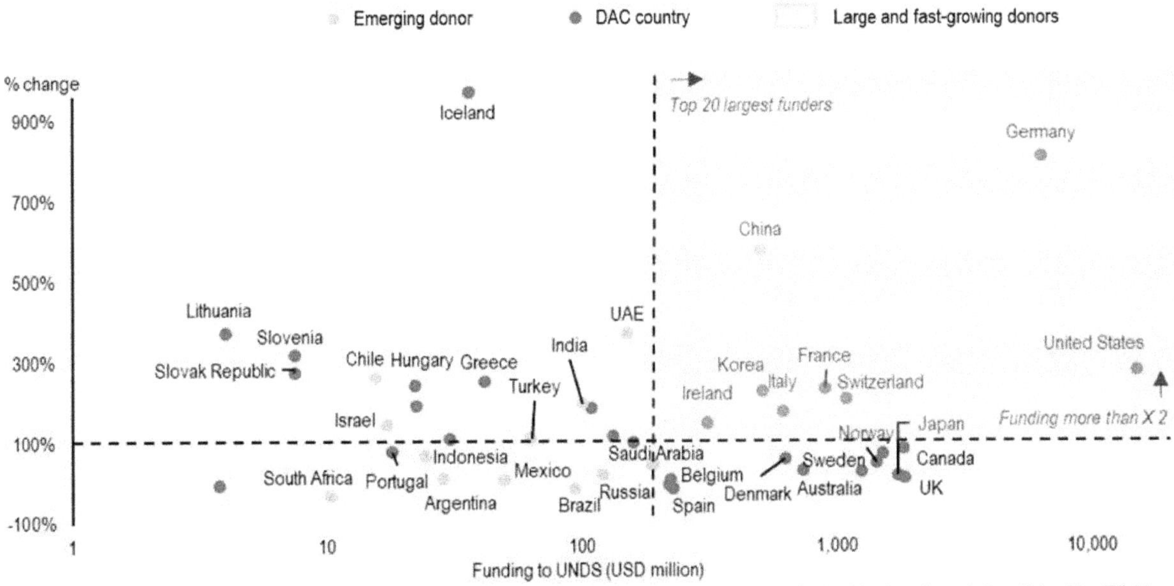


Note: Emerging donors include Brazil, Russia, India, China, South Africa, Indonesia, Argentina, Chile, Mexico, Israel, Saudi Arabia, Türkiye, and the United Arab Emirates (Hughes and Mitchell, 2023[13]). Calculations include core assessed, core voluntary and non-core (earmarked) contributions provided by government donors but exclude non-core local resources.
Source: Authors' calculations based on UNSCEB (2024[14]), *Financial Statistics*, https://unsceb.org/financial-statistics.

StatLink https://stat.link/t6gr0m

**Emerging donors are increasingly leveraging the "power of the purse" to secure influence in the UNDS.** Funding serves as a mechanism for countries to assert their influence, and the highest contributions from emerging donors to specific UN entities reveal their strategic priorities. For instance, China's largest contributions go to the UN Secretariat and the Food and Agriculture Organization (FAO), while its earmarked funding prioritises the UN Department for Economic and Social Affairs (UN DESA). This is consistent with China's objective of securing high-level UN senior management positions: Chinese nationals currently lead both UN DESA and the FAO. Similarly, Saudi Arabia focuses its contributions on the World Food Program (WFP) and the United Nations Relief and Works Agency for Palestine Refugees in the Near East (UNRWA), and the United Arab Emirates targets the WFP and FAO, reflecting their emphasis on humanitarian assistance and support for the Middle East region. Funding practices are also increasingly wielded as an instrument of soft power and diplomatic leverage. This was notably exemplified in 2020 when China publicly criticised the United States for its funding arrears, highlighting the geopolitical dimensions that multilateral funding practices can assume (Fung and Lam, 2022[15]).

## Financing from the multilateral development system (outflows)

### *Multilateral outflows remain resilient despite multiple shocks and crises*

**Multilateral outflows rebounded in 2022 after a temporary decline in 2021.** In 2022, multilateral outflows amounted to USD 259 billion, reflecting a 12% increase on the previous year (Figure 1.8). This recovery followed a 12% decrease in 2021, which saw subdued outflows after an exceptional expansion in financing to combat the COVID-19 crisis in 2020, reaching the record level of USD 264 billion. Of the total outflows in 2022, USD 46 billion (18%) were earmarked, while USD 213 billion (82%) were from multilateral organisations' core resources. As discussed in Chapter 2, a significant part of the increase in multilateral development finance between 2021 and 2022 can be attributed to heightened support for Ukraine.

#### Figure 1.8. Multilateral outflows have rebounded and are close to reaching 2020's peak levels

Evolution of multilateral outflows from core and earmarked resources, 2012-22

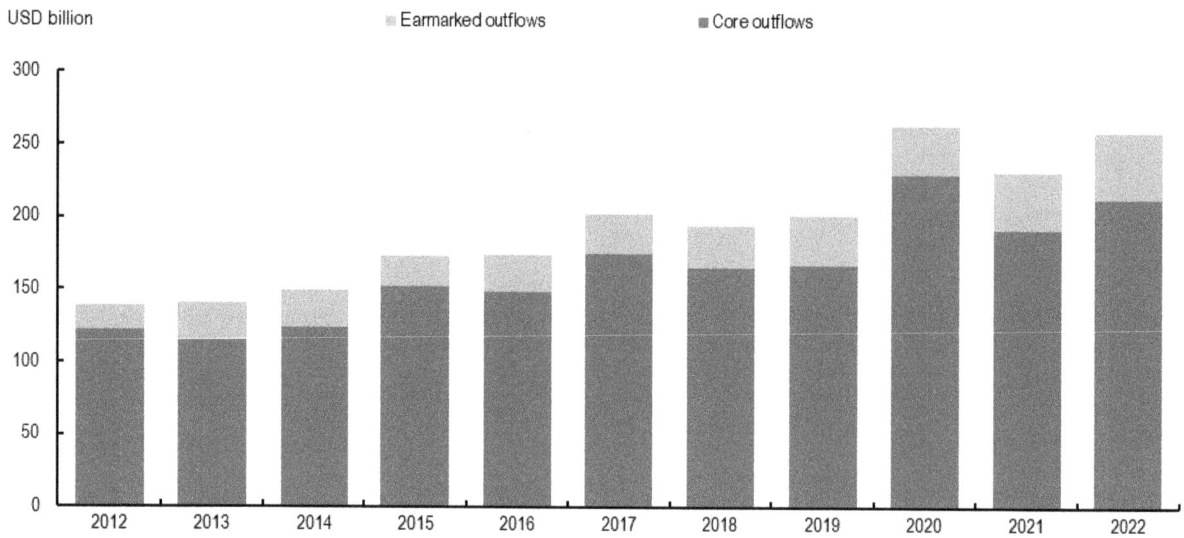


Note: Calculations are based on commitments, in 2022 constant prices.
Source: Authors' calculations based on OECD (2024[3]), OECD Data Explorer, *Creditor Reporting System* (database), http://data-explorer.oecd.org/s/c.

StatLink https://stat.link/tj540h

**Multilateral organisations have been swift to adapt their sectoral allocations in response to successive crises.** The previous edition of this report stressed the ability of multilateral organisations to pivot their support towards health and social protection during the COVID-19 pandemic, highlighting their flexibility and versatility (OECD, 2022[10]). This capacity to adapt to changing circumstances was again evident in 2021 and 2022, this time in response to the impact of Russia's war of aggression against Ukraine (Figure 1.9). For example, the share of humanitarian aid increased from 7% in 2020 to 10% in 2021 and 13% in 2022. This reflected the change in priorities of multilateral organisations, as they shifted their pandemic focus from public health and social protection towards humanitarian crisis response. Notably, budget support stands out as a versatile modality to help countries weather budgetary issues created by different crises. Multilateral outflows for governance interventions, which includes budget support, registered a significant rise (from 11% to 17%) between 2019 and 2020, as the multilateral development system supported developing countries during the first year of the COVID-19 pandemic. After decreasing to 13% in 2021, it increased again to 16% in 2022, as multilateral channels were used to offer budgetary relief to Ukraine.

## Figure 1.9. Multilateral organisations adjust their sectoral allocations to tackle successive crises

Sector distribution of multilateral outflows (core and earmarked), 2019-22

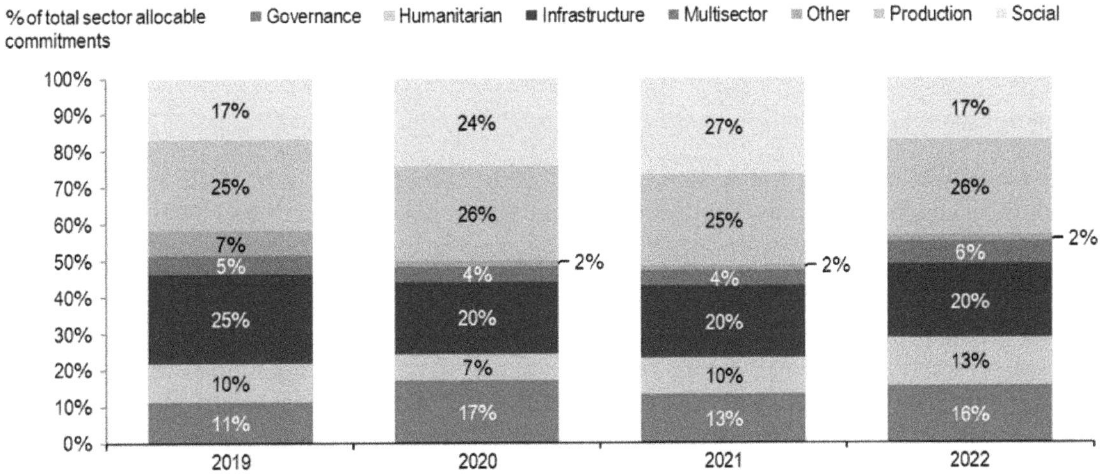


Note: Share of total sector allocable multilateral core and earmarked commitments, in 2022 constant prices.
Source: Authors' calculations based on OECD (2024[3]), OECD Data Explorer, *Creditor Reporting System* (database), http://data-explorer.oecd.org/s/c.

StatLink https://stat.link/t7lk60

### *Multilateral organisations are venturing beyond traditional mandates to tackle new priorities*

**In addition to their traditional mandates, multilateral organisations are stepping up to address new priorities of the financing for sustainable development agenda.** These include (1) new efforts to mobilise largely untapped financing sources, such as private finance, to unlock additional resources for developing countries; and (2) enhancing their contributions to frontier areas in development financing, such as climate finance.

#### *Multilateral providers lead efforts to mobilise private finance, but more is needed*

**Multilateral organisations have become the principal actors in private finance mobilisation.** In 2022, multilateral providers mobilised USD 47 billion in private finance, compared to 14 USD billion mobilised by DAC members. The share of multilateral actors in the total amounts mobilised increased from 67% in 2015 to 77% in 2022. Among the multilateral organisations, private finance mobilisation is primarily led by the MDBs and EU institutions. Between 2020 and 2022, the International Finance Corporation (IFC), Inter-American Development Bank (IADB), Multilateral Investment Guarantee Agency (MIGA) and the EU institutions mobilised the largest amounts of private finance. Despite significant progress, multilateral organisations face mounting pressure to enhance their mobilisation efforts. The total amount mobilised from both multilateral and DAC providers in 2022, USD 62 billion, is still far short of the G20 IEG's annual target of USD 240 billion by 2030 (G20 IEG, 2023[16]). In addition, existing mechanisms have demonstrated their limitations in rapidly scaling up private finance. For example, the International Development Association's (IDA) Private Sector Window got off to a slow start, using only half of its initial envelope, although the pace of project approvals has recently picked up.

**As for the other MDB reform areas, a focus on expanding the use of financing instruments will not be sufficient to overcome all the obstacles to mobilising private finance.** Research has shown that investment challenges in the poorest and most vulnerable countries stem from a combination of national-level factors, including political instability and high indebtedness, and project-level risks such as high project preparation costs. It is thus important, while backing MDBs' efforts, to recognise the limitations in terms of scalability of such project-based approaches. There are also doubts about the value for money and additionality of interventions that use scarce concessional resources to subsidise private investments. This situation calls for clear criteria to explicitly and consciously evaluate the benefits and costs of designing blended finance initiatives, especially in least developed countries and other challenging contexts.

*Multilateral climate finance has grown, but enhancing its scale and focus is challenging*

**Multilateral organisations are increasingly embracing climate action in their mandates.** MDBs' climate-related development finance surged by nearly 300% between 2013 and 2022, from USD 16.4 billion to USD 65.2 billion. The share of operations dedicated to climate finance grew from about 15% of their total operations in 2015 to 24% in 2022 (Mitchell and Wickstead, 2024[17]).

**Multilateral organisations need to change their models to improve climate support.** Despite greater multilateral focus on climate action, meeting the growing needs in this area will require both more financing and better targeting. The current levels of financing fall short of the ambitious climate goals set by the international community. The United Nations Framework Convention on Climate Change's notes that developing countries require at least USD 6 trillion by 2030 to meet less than half of their existing Nationally Determined Contributions (UNFCCC Standing Committee on Finance, 2021[18]). However, there are also significant disparities in the allocation of funds, with insufficient resources directed towards the most vulnerable, such as adaptation efforts in low-income countries.

### *Tensions are rising as organisations juggle their traditional roles with new mandates and responsibilities*

**The multilateral development system's capacity to address poverty mainly relies on its concessional, donor-funded facilities.** The fight against poverty has historically been a central focus of multilateral development concessional finance, with many multilateral organisations' mandates dedicated to poverty reduction. Figure 1.10, Panel A suggests that multilateral organisations' outflows have a stronger focus on poverty than bilateral donors', leveraging their ability to provide concessional finance to the poorest and most vulnerable countries. Multilateral providers' stronger poverty and inequality focus is also evident in their sectoral allocations, which target greater portions of their development finance to social sectors than do bilateral donors (Figure 1.10, Panel B).

**Figure 1.10. Multilateral organisations are able to focus on poverty through concessional finance**

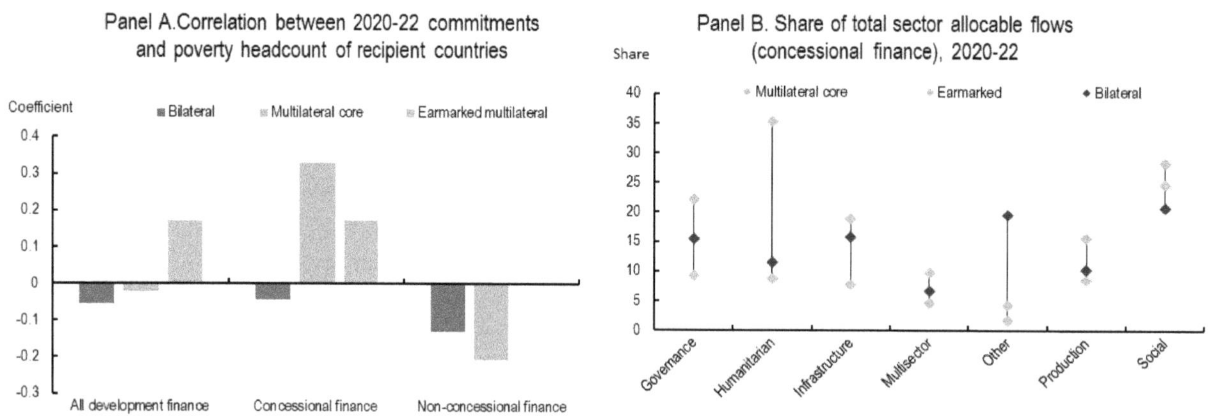


Note: In Panel B, calculations are based on commitments, in 2022 constant prices.
Source: Authors' calculations based on OECD (2024[3]), OECD Data Explorer, *Creditor Reporting System* (database), http://data-explorer.oecd.org/s/c; World Bank Group (2024[19]), *World Development Indicators* (database), https://databank.worldbank.org/source/world-development-indicators.

StatLink https://stat.link/k2evna

**If not managed properly, the trade-off between scale and concessionality could end up limiting multilateral organisations' poverty focus.** Typically, organisations that exclusively provide concessional finance tend to commit fewer financial resources overall than those that provide both concessional and non-concessional finance. Figure 1.11 traces the change in the share of concessional finance and the overall volume of multilateral organisations' financing between 2013-2015 and 2020-2022. It reveals that most organisations increased the size of their financial commitments during this period, some significantly. However, many of these organisations also reduced the proportion of concessional finance within their total commitments.

### Figure 1.11. Many multilateral organisations that increase financing tend to reduce the share of concessional finance

Change in outflows and change in share of concessional finance, 2013-15 versus 2020-22

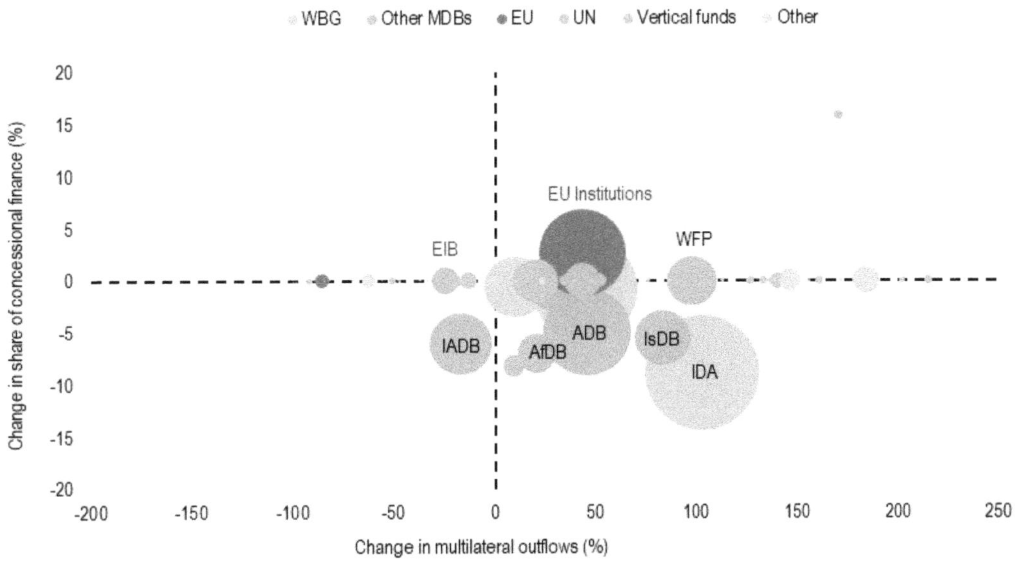


Note: Calculations are based on commitments, in 2022 constant prices. ADB: Asian Development Bank; AfDB: African Development Bank; EIB: European Investment Bank; IADB: Inter-American Development Bank; IDA: International Development Association; IsDB: Islamic Development Bank; WFP: World Food Programme. Bubble size represents volume of outflows.
Source: Authors' calculations based on OECD (2024[3]), OECD Data Explorer, *Creditor Reporting System* (database), http://data-explorer.oecd.org/s/c.

StatLink https://stat.link/z3870b

**The continued reliance on financial innovation is likely to tilt the balance further towards non-concessional resources, which are typically less well suited to fighting poverty.** In particular, multilateral reforms focused on optimising MDB balance sheets could undermine their ability to effectively target poverty-relevant sectors and support the poorest and most vulnerable countries if not complemented by efforts to stock up their concessional resources.

## Towards a future-fit multilateral development system

**This report has identified three gradual yet long-running shifts in multilateral development finance.** These shifts fall into three broad areas: (1) expansion; (2) diversification; and (3) fragmentation. They have implications for all the aspects of multilateral development finance examined in this report: the multilateral architecture and reform processes (Chapter 2), funding to the multilateral system (inflows) (Chapter 3), and financing from the multilateral system (outflows) (Chapter 4). Figure 1.12 summarises these shifts and their implications.

**Figure 1.12. Three deep currents – of expansion, diversification and fragmentation – are gradually changing the face of multilateral development finance**

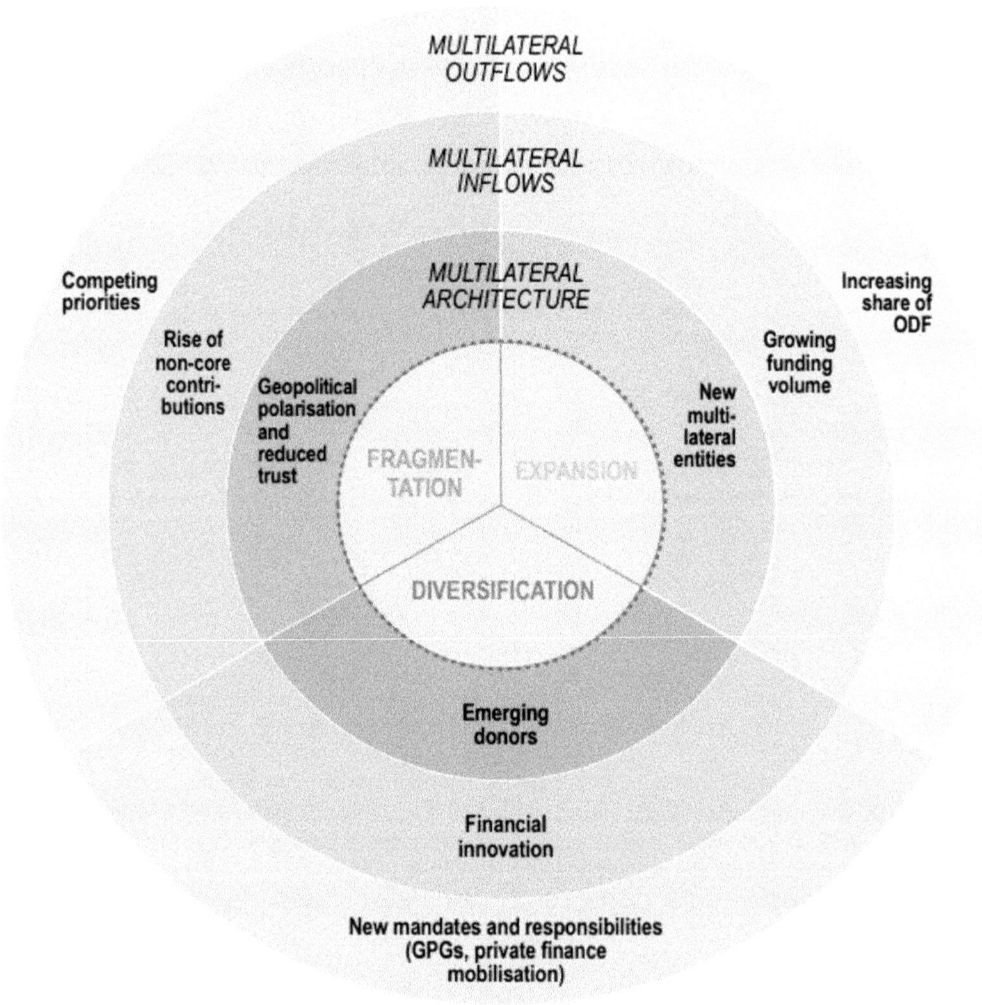


Against this backdrop, the report puts forward policy recommendations to make multilateral development finance fit for the future. These recommendations aim to equip multilateral organisations to fulfil their original mandates while also developing the capacity to address emerging challenges and manage trade-offs. The common thread running through these recommendations is the goal of balancing the efficiency-driven measures of ongoing reforms with a re-emphasis on multilateral effectiveness:

### *Multilateral architecture and reform process*

- **Prioritise rationalising the multilateral architecture in global discussions:** Make the systemic issues related to the expansion and fragmentation of the multilateral architecture a key agenda item in global fora, such as the Fourth Financing for Development (FfD4) Conference and G20 meetings. Engage the heads of major IFIs, UN agencies, multilateral funds and key official providers (e.g. G20 members) in this effort to provide guidance and co-ordinate actions according to their respective mandates. Promote and support global initiatives aimed at rationalising the multilateral architecture, especially in crowded sectors such as multilateral climate finance.

- **Promote greater collaboration in multilateral reforms:** Ensure a collaborative approach to MDB and UN reforms. Use existing fora to share experiences and lessons from individual organisations engaged in reform processes to benefit the broader system and avoid a siloed approach to multilateral reforms. Opportunities for MDB learning include the AfDB's transformation of country engagement, as well as EBRD's experience in private finance mobilisation. Similarly, UNDS entities can learn from the successes and challenges of ongoing special agency reforms, such as the World Health Organization.
- **Ensure coherence in multilateral development co-operation through whole-of-government approaches:** Strengthen dialogue among government functions (aid agencies, treasuries, ministries of foreign affairs) on cross-cutting multilateral issues, such as the MDB reform. This can ensure coherence and balance between financial considerations promoted by treasuries and the focus on development impact central to foreign relations and aid agencies' missions.
- **Harmonise donor requirements:** Address the lack of standardisation in bilateral and multilateral donors' reporting requirements to reduce the burden on multilateral organisations and recipient countries:
    - Use discussions in the governing body of each organisation to agree on common reporting needs from bilateral donors. This is increasingly important given the growing role of emerging donors, which could otherwise impose additional burdens on multilateral organisations.
    - Ensure multilateral organisations and funds harmonise their requirements to reduce transaction costs in accessing multilateral funds for recipient countries and mitigate the impact of donor proliferation.
- **Bring aid effectiveness principles to scale:** With close to half of ODA channelled through the multilateral system, it is important that the effectiveness principles adopted by bilateral donors – country ownership, focus on results, inclusive partnerships, transparency and mutual accountability – are not lost in the new global financing architecture. Reinvigorate the dialogue among and between multilateral and bilateral providers to operationalise and monitor the implementation of these principles in multilateral development co-operation.

### *Funding to the multilateral development system (inflows)*

- **Maximise contributions to high-impact funding mechanisms:** Capitalise on the multiplier effect of multilateral funding mechanisms to achieve initial reform targets by ensuring successful replenishments of MDB concessional windows and global funds. Explore the possibility of additional capital contributions (e.g. to general capital increases or hybrid capital instruments). Ensure that a substantial portion of multilateral development finance remains highly concessional and affordable for the poorest and most vulnerable countries.
- **Ensure adequate funding for core strategic functions:** Invest in the core functions of multilateral organisations to maintain their ability to perform their mandates. Adjust the formula and level of UN assessed contributions to reflect member countries' actual economic weight. This can ensure increased, fair share contributions, and help rebalance core and earmarked contributions to the UNDS. Recognising the specificities of each multilateral organisation, bring discussions on funding quality to their governing bodies to complement general UN Funding Compact commitments (following the model of the WHO reform or structured financing dialogues).
- **Prioritise flexible funding:** In accordance with UN Funding Compact commitments, prioritise multi-year and flexible funding modalities, such as contributions to multi-donor and inter-agency

pooled funds, as these foster co-ordination, reduce fragmentation and enable organisations to adapt to countries' needs.

- **Engage with emerging donors on multilateral development finance:** Acknowledge the growing role of some non-DAC donors in the multilateral system. Use existing OECD DAC outreach mechanisms, such as the policy dialogues with Arab, Latin American and Caribbean countries, to discuss insights from OECD analysis on multilateral development finance and effective multilateral development co-operation and to develop common ground for good practices in these areas.

### *Financing from the multilateral development system (outflows)*

- **Safeguard the system's capacity to support the poorest and most vulnerable:** Preserve multilateral organisations' capacity to target poverty-relevant sectors and support the poorest and most vulnerable countries by monitoring the impact of their reforms and increasing their concessional resources.
    - Commission an assessment through the G20 or another relevant global forum to understand the impacts of recent and ongoing reforms on aid allocation across sectors, regions and country groupings.
    - Complement efforts to increase MDBs' financial leverage with measures to stock up their concessional resources, reversing the decade-long trend of stagnation in donor contributions.
- **Promote greater complementarity of multilateral aid portfolios:** Support research on multilateral aid portfolios at the sectoral and country levels, such as OECD portfolio similarity analyses, to inform multilateral reforms and programming. This can contribute to greater transparency, coherence and co-ordination among multilateral activities by clarifying their complementarity in terms of sector, geography and instrument.
- **Catalyse private investment:** Build on, and learn from, innovative portfolio approaches to tap into different sources of private finance, including institutional investors. Adopt clear criteria to evaluate the additionality and opportunity costs of blended finance initiatives, especially in least developed countries and other challenging contexts. Support a greater role for multilateral organisations in creating an environment conducive to private investment at the country level, such as by supporting initiatives to address risk misperceptions, to complement the current focus on deploying financial instruments at the project level.
- **Accelerate climate efforts in high-impact areas:** Ensure the additionality of multilateral climate finance and development finance, such as by targeting win-win investments to support country-led strategies. This includes strengthening efforts to expand adaptation finance, including by mainstreaming climate into sectors beyond infrastructure and production. Ensure climate diagnostics are embedded into country strategy and results frameworks. Improve and standardise climate reporting to rigorously assess the climate contribution of projects ex-ante and ex-post. Enhance co-ordination among multilateral and bilateral development partners through joint monitoring and knowledge work, including through country platforms.

## References


African Development Bank et al. (2024), *MDBs Working as a System for Impact and Scale*, https://www.iadb.org/document.cfm?id=EZIDB0000577-986313001-135 (accessed on July 2024). [6]

Fung, C. and S. Lam (2022), *Mixed report card: China's influence at the United Nations*, Blog, Lowy Institute, https://www.lowyinstitute.org/publications/mixed-report-card-china-s-influence-united-nations. [15]

G20 IEG (2023), *Strengthening Multilateral Development Banks: The Triple Agenda*, https://www.cgdev.org/sites/default/files/The_Triple_Agenda_G20-IEG_Report_Volume1_2023.pdf. [16]

Government of Barbados (2022), *The 2022 Bridgetown Initiative for the Reform of the Global Financial Architecture*, https://pmo.gov.bb/wp-content/uploads/2022/10/The-2022-Bridgetown-Initiative.pdf. [5]

Hughes, S. and I. Mitchell (2023), *Emerging Actors in the Multilateral System*, Center for Global Development, https://www.cgdev.org/publication/emerging-actors-multilateral-system. [13]

Kenny, C. and S. Morris (2021), *A Climate-Dedicated Capital Increase at the World Bank and IFC*, Center for Global Development, https://www.cgdev.org/publication/climate-dedicated-capital-increase-world-bank-and-ifc. [12]

Mitchell, I. and E. Wickstead (2024), *Has the $100 billion climate goal been reached?*, Center for Global Development, https://www.cgdev.org/publication/has-100-billion-climate-goal-been-reached. [17]

OECD (2024), *Creditor Reporting System (database)*, http://data-explorer.oecd.org/s/c (accessed on 22 April 2024). [3]

OECD (2024), *DAC1 Table*, http://data-explorer.oecd.org/s/t (accessed on 22 April 2024). [2]

OECD (2024), *Members' total use of the multilateral system*, http://data-explorer.oecd.org/s/s (accessed on 22 April 2024). [8]

OECD (2022), *Multilateral Development Finance 2022*, OECD Publishing, Paris, https://doi.org/10.1787/9fea4cf2-en. [10]

OECD (2020), *Multilateral Development Finance 2020*, OECD Publishing, Paris, https://doi.org/10.1787/e61fdf00-en. [1]

OECD (2015), *Multilateral Aid 2015: Better Partnerships for a Post-2015 World*, OECD Publishing, Paris, https://doi.org/10.1787/9789264235212-en. [9]

UNFCCC Standing Committee on Finance (2021), *First report on the determination of the needs of developing country Parties related to implementing the Convention and the Paris Agreement*. [18]

United Nations (2024), *Funding Compact for the United Nations' Support to the Sustainable Development Goals*, https://unsdg.un.org/sites/default/files/2024-06/Funding%20compact_280524.pdf. [7]

UNSCEB (2024), *Financial Statistics*, https://unsceb.org/financial-statistics. [14]

US Department of State (2022), *Remarks by Secretary of the Treasury Janet L. Yellen at the Center for Global Development*, https://home.treasury.gov/news/press-releases/jy0997. [4]

World Bank Group (2024), *IDA - Contributor countries*, https://ida.worldbank.org/en/about/contributor-countries. [11]

World Bank Group (2024), *World Development Indicators (database)*, https://databank.worldbank.org/source/world-development-indicators (accessed on April 2024). [19]

## Notes

[1] African Development Bank (AfDB); Asian Development Bank (ADB); Asian Infrastructure Investment Bank (AIIB); Council of Europe Development Bank (CEB); European Bank for Reconstruction and Development (EBRD); European Investment Bank (EIB); Inter-American Development Bank (IDB); Islamic Development Bank (IsDB); New Development Bank (NDB); World Bank Group (WBG)

[2] Hybrid capital instruments are financial instruments that have both debt and equity properties. Such instruments are specifically designed to be subordinated to other types of debt and may be written off to absorb losses.

# 2 High stakes amid high risks: reforming multilateral development co-operation in a changing world

This chapter provides an overview of the global context surrounding and influencing the evolution of multilateral development finance, including the challenging economic and financial environment facing developing countries. It describes the increasing relevance of the multilateral development system in the development landscape, its current limitations and efforts by multilateral stakeholders to make it fit for future challenges. While emphasising that multilateral organisations are at the forefront of reforming the global financial architecture, the chapter argues that these reforms can only succeed with a robust multilateral development system, underscoring the need to balance efficiency-focused reforms with effectiveness considerations.

## Multilateral finance is increasingly central in the development co-operation landscape

### *The multilateral development system delivers the majority of official development finance to developing countries*

**Since its inception in the aftermath of the Second World War, the multilateral development system has expanded to include over 200 multilateral entities.** These organisations, varying in form, mandate and size, form a multi-faceted web of institutions, funding and delivery mechanisms, often referred to as the multilateral development system. Over time, this composite architecture has evolved to adapt to new realities and needs. A previous edition of this report described the system's gradual transformation since its inception after the Second World War in response to successive crises and development challenges, underscoring the system's adaptive and expansive nature (OECD, 2020[1]). While there are multiple ways to classify multilateral organisations, this report groups them into four broad categories: (i) entities that are part of the United Nations Development System (UNDS), (ii) multilateral development banks (MDBs), (iii) vertical funds and (iv) other multilateral organisations.

**The multilateral development system is a core component of the global aid architecture.** Multilateral organisations are key platforms for orchestrating collective responses to global development challenges such as poverty, climate change, and public health crises. They are also instrumental in delivering official development finance to developing countries (Figure 2.1). Thanks to their leverage capacity, some multilateral actors, such as the MDBs, are able to provide significantly more financing to ODA-eligible countries than the contributions they receive from donors.

**Figure 2.1. Multilateral organisations are an essential link in the development assistance chain**

Total flows by type of multilateral organisation, commitments, in billion USD, 2012-22

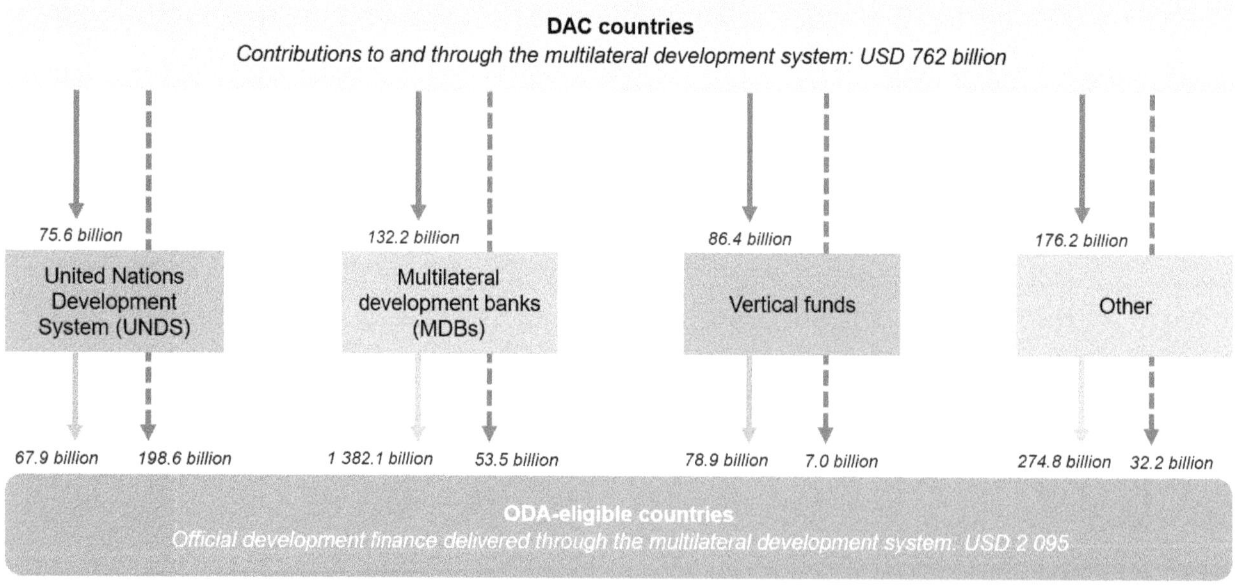


Note: Cumulative totals in USD billion, at 2022 constant prices. Grey non-dashed arrows represent core contributions to multilateral organisations (multilateral ODA). Grey dashed arrows correspond to DAC countries' contributions earmarked through multilateral organisations (multi-bi aid or non-core contributions), which include both ODA and other official flows (OOF). Coloured arrows represent multilateral organisations' outflows, which include concessional and non-concessional flows.

Source: OECD (2024[2]), OECD Data Explorer, *Creditor Reporting System* (database), http://data-explorer.oecd.org/s/c.

**The comparative advantages and shortcomings of multilateral development cooperation are a subject of continuous debate.** Previous editions of this report have outlined some of the main reasons DAC members choose to channel their aid through the multilateral system, including economies of scale, financial leverage, geographical reach, specialised expertise, and political legitimacy (OECD, 2020[1]; OECD, 2022[3]). Multilateral development finance plays a critical role in promoting sustainable development and provides vital support during crises, offering a countercyclical source of financing to help countries withstand external shocks. Through their normative role, multilateral organisations also promote governance based on global standards and encourage international co-operation. On the other hand, criticisms of the multilateral development system often highlight its institutional complexity, perceived lack of transparency and accountability, and high administrative costs. Ultimately, the key consideration is whether the efficiency gains from pooling resources and leveraging the system's comparative advantages outweigh concerns over costs, accountability and control.

**Approximately two-thirds of official development finance is provided by, or channelled through, multilateral organisations.** These organisations have the extensive reach and capacity to implement programmes across multiple countries and sectors, making them indispensable for delivering on the global sustainable development agenda. Between 2012 and 2022, the "market share" of the multilateral development system in total official development finance (ODF) extended to ODA-eligible countries grew by 36%, from 45% to 61% (Figure 2.2). The substantial share of official development finance delivered by, or through, multilateral organisations underscores the international community's reliance on these institutions to support developing countries. As examined in Chapters 3 and 4, the growth of multilateral outflows as a share of total ODF reflects both the increase in donors' funding to multilateral organisations, and the growing use of MDBs' capacity to leverage their resources by tapping into the capital markets.

## Figure 2.2. The "market share" of the multilateral development system has grown by 36% over the past ten years

Evolution of the share of official development finance (ODF) delivered by the multilateral system, 2012 versus 2022

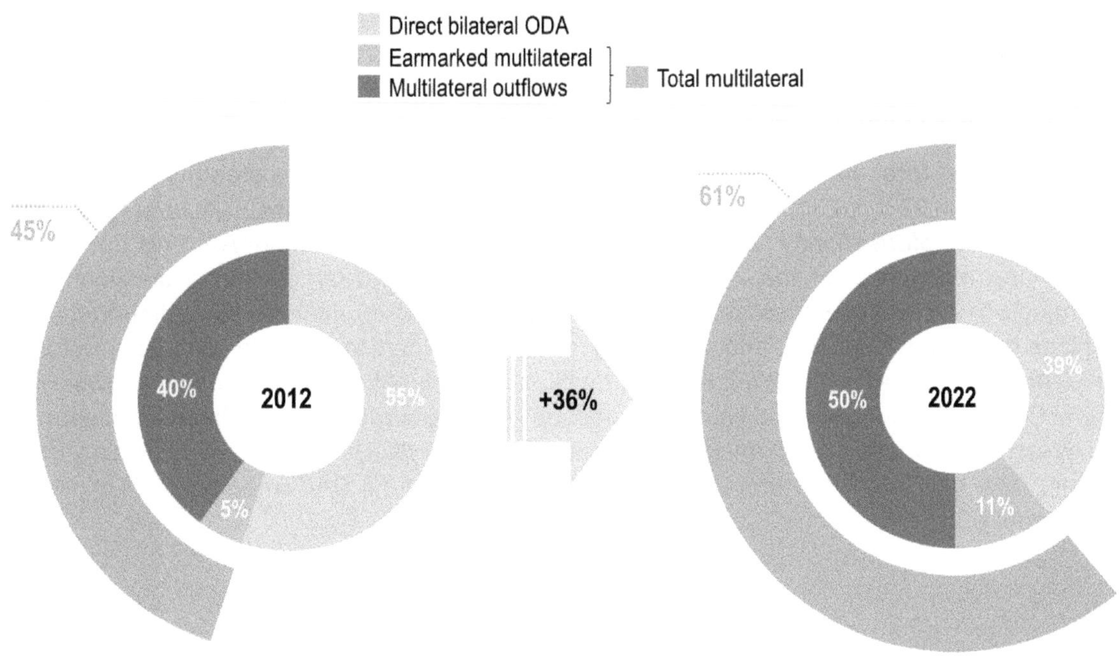


Note: Official development finance (ODF) corresponds to the sum of concessional and non-concessional resources from official bilateral and multilateral sources.
Source: OECD (2024[2]), OECD Data Explorer, *Creditor Reporting System* (database), http://data-explorer.oecd.org/s/c.

### *By the early 2030s, the multilateral system could become the predominant channel of DAC members' ODA*

**Multilateral organisations rely on financial contributions from their members to deliver on their mandates.** Although there is a variety of multilateral organisations with different funding models and sources – including public donations and philanthropic contributions – members and shareholders represent a vital source of funding. In many organisations, these donor contributions are essential for sustaining core corporate functions and activities, and for pursuing the agendas and strategic directions established by their governing boards.

**Multilateral ODA embodies the essence of investing in multilateral action.** The term multilateral ODA refers to core financial contributions provided by donor governments to ODA-eligible multilateral organisations. This type of funding does not specify which projects and programmes are to be funded. Instead, these resources become an integral part of multilateral organisations' financial assets and can be used to fulfil their core mandates within the parameters set by their governing board. These core resources are essential as they provide the financial foundation of most multilateral organisations. Their unearmarked nature allows multilateral organisations to decide strategically on the best possible use of these resources, ensuring they can respond effectively and flexibly to countries' evolving needs.

**The members and shareholders of multilateral organisations also allocate resources that are earmarked for specific purposes.** In addition to their multilateral ODA, many donors provide multilateral organisations with non-core contributions assigned to specific sectors, themes, countries or regions. These earmarked resources, officially reported as bilateral ODA (also referred to as non-core contributions or multi-bi aid), allow donors to target their contributions more precisely and maintain greater control over their allocations. Despite being less predictable, these earmarked contributions are an important means for bilateral donors to respond to emerging crises or target specific geographic and thematic areas. Chapter 3 delves further into the trends, advantages and disadvantages of both core and non-core contributions to the multilateral development system.

**Multilateral organisations play a more significant role in the international aid architecture than core contributions alone might suggest.** The sum of core and non-core contributions constitutes official providers' total use of the multilateral system. This combined total offers a more comprehensive indication of how donors use the multilateral development system, since it takes into account all types of funding provided to, or channelled through, multilateral organisations.

**OECD DAC members' total use of the multilateral development system has steadily increased over the past decade.** From 37% in 2010, the share of ODA channelled to or through multilateral organisations rose to 45% in 2021, before slightly declining to 43% in 2022 (Figure 2.3, Panel A.). This upward trend reflects a growing recognition of the value of the multilateral system for delivering development co-operation projects to support countries' sustainable development. It also underscores the importance DAC members place on pooling resources and leveraging multilateral expertise to tackle complex development challenges. The slight decline in the 2022 share of multilateral contributions is due both to a lower volume of multilateral ODA — following several years of increases — and a surge in direct bilateral and earmarked aid, driven by increased support for Ukraine and in-donor refugee costs. Despite this slight decline, if recent trends persist, the multilateral system could channel nearly half of DAC members' ODA by 2030 (Figure 2.3, Panel B.).

### Figure 2.3. The long-run trend shows a slow but steady increase in the use of the multilateral system

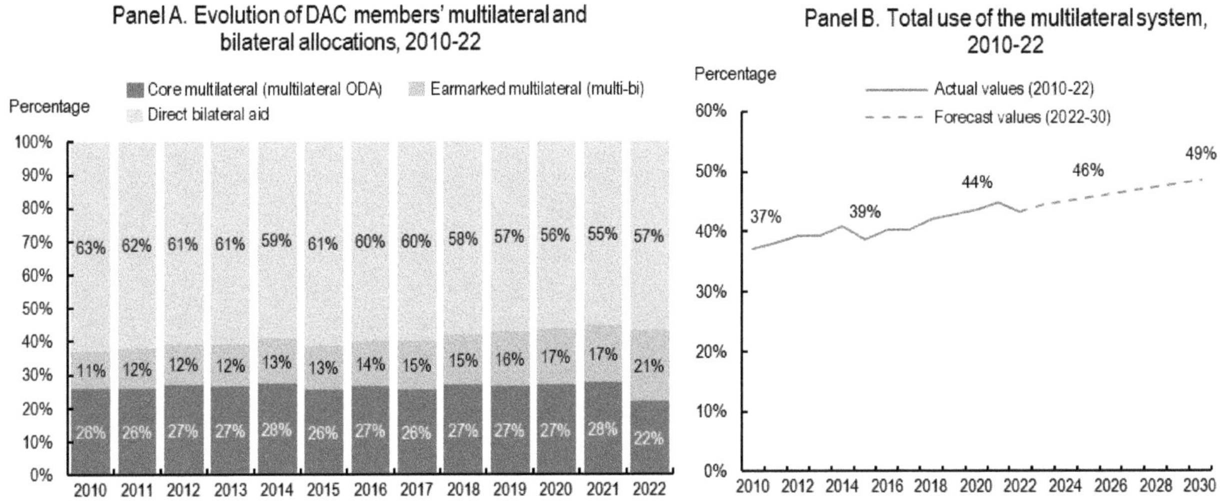


Note: Direct bilateral ODA refers to DAC members' bilateral ODA excluding multi-bi aid (non-core contributions to multilateral organisations). Calculations are based on gross disbursements in 2022 constant prices. In Panel B, values beyond 2022 are calculated using a linear forecast.
Source: Authors' calculations based on OECD (2024[2]), OECD Data Explorer, *DAC1 table*, http://data-explorer.oecd.org/s/t.

**Bilateral partners' use of the multilateral system can be an important factor in their ability to fulfil ODA-related commitments.** All countries that meet the UN target of spending 0.7% of their gross national income (GNI) on ODA make more significant use of the multilateral system than the DAC average. Specifically, these countries allocate more than 40% of their ODA to or through multilateral organisations (Figure 2.4). However, not all countries that make significant use of the multilateral system are close to meeting the 0.7% ODA/GNI target. This indicates that while the multilateral system can be a valuable conduit for delivering additional ODA, making significant use of the multilateral system is not sufficient to achieve this target without strong political leadership and commitment. Nevertheless, this finding does suggest that DAC countries aiming to close their gap to the target should consider how multilateral development co-operation can contribute.

**Figure 2.4. All DAC countries that meet the 0.7% of ODA/GNI target make significant use of the multilateral system**

DAC countries' ODA as percent of GNI and total use of the multilateral system as percent of total ODA excluding contributions to EU Institutions, 2022

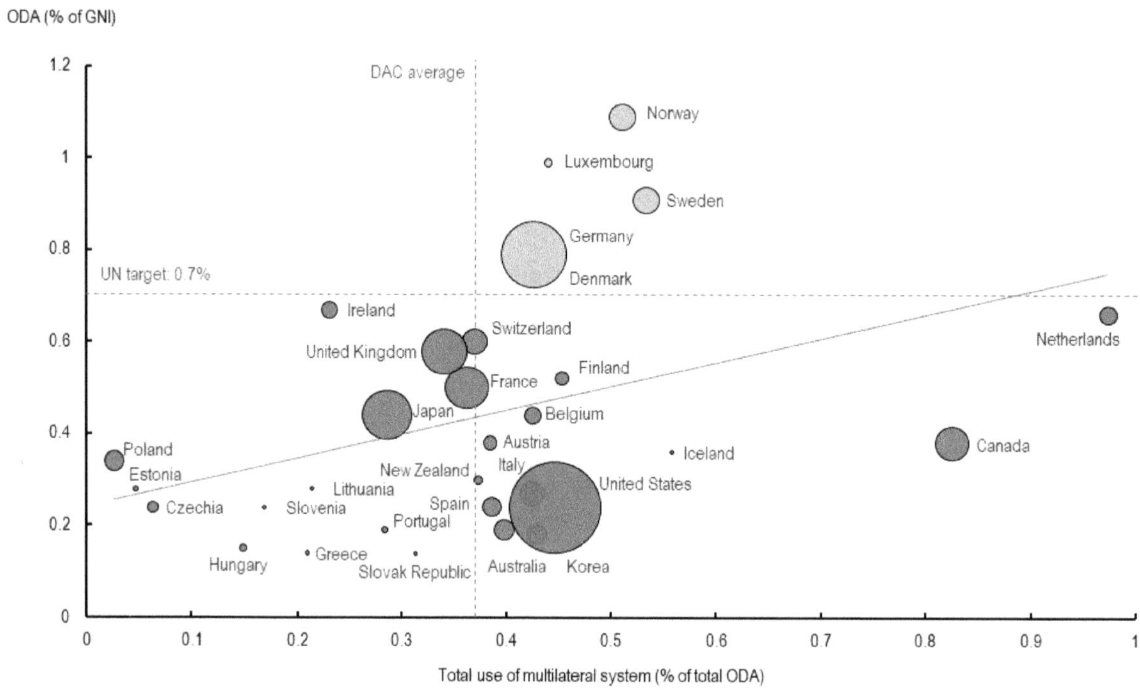


Note: The size of the bubbles reflects each country's volume of total ODA, excluding contributions to EU Institutions.
Source: OECD (2024[2]), OECD Data Explorer, *Creditor Reporting System* (database), http://data-explorer.oecd.org/s/c.

**Given the growing importance of the multilateral system in development co-operation, monitoring and analysing aid flows to, and from, the multilateral development system is an essential task.** As the main shareholders and funders of the multilateral development system, DAC members have an inherent interest in ensuring that the resources channelled through the system are used effectively and invested where they can achieve the greatest results. Examining and analysing these flows provides a bird's-eye view of the functioning of the multilateral development system and sheds light on the impact of public resources channelled to and through it. OECD DAC statistics on aid flows to and from the multilateral development system, described in Box 2.1, are a key source of multilateral development finance data.

**Box 2.1. The role of the OECD's Creditor Reporting System in tracking official providers' use of the multilateral system**

**The OECD DAC's Creditor Reporting System (CRS) maintains official statistics on aid flows to, and from, the multilateral development system.** DAC members and other official providers report to the OECD their contributions to, and through, the multilateral development system as part of an annual data cycle. These flows of DAC members and other official providers' funding to the multilateral development system are examined in Chapter 3. Multilateral organisations, in turn, report their outflows to the OECD, including details on the allocation of these resources by recipient, sector and purpose. Chapter 4 analyses the financing flows from the multilateral development system, including multilateral outflows from these organisations' core resources and earmarked aid channelled by bilateral providers through multilateral organisations.

**OECD DAC statistics are continuously being improved to provide a more complete and accurate picture of multilateral development finance.** Through its Working Party on Development Finance Statistics, the OECD DAC monitors and regularly reviews the statistical standards of development finance, including those pertinent to multilateral development finance. A significant recent improvement was the incorporation of new co-operation modalities into the CRS in 2022. This makes it possible to distinguish between single and multi-donor funding mechanisms, allowing for more granular statistics on donor contributions to multilateral organisations (DAC Working Party on Development Finance Statistics, 2023[4]). Additionally, the annual revision of the list of ODA-eligible international organisations remains crucial in ensuring the accuracy and relevance of multilateral development finance statistics (OECD, 2024[5]).

Note: The Creditor Reporting System and other OECD DAC statistics can be accessed on the OECD Data Explorer, OECD (2024[6]), http://data-explorer.oecd.org.

### *The challenging context underscores both the relevance and limitations of multilateral development finance*

**Multilateral development finance offers critical support to economies struggling with the impacts of global economic slowdowns and financial market volatility.** In the current high-risk post-pandemic context, characterised by rising debt and high capital costs facing developing countries, multilateral institutions play a crucial role in mobilising resources to help countries maintain financial stability. In particular, their ability to channel significant volumes of concessional resources to developing countries makes them an essential source of affordable finance.

**While lending from multilateral creditors provides developing countries with a crucial lifeline in times of crisis, it was unable to fully offset the outflows of private capital experienced in 2022** (Diwan and Songwe, 2024[7]). Long-term debt from official creditors, especially multilateral ones, offers a stable and countercyclical source of financing. Over the past decade, net inflows from multilateral creditors to developing countries have consistently remained positive and relatively stable (Figure 2.5). Despite this, they were insufficient to counterbalance the substantial private capital outflows in 2022, which totalled USD 189.4 billion (World Bank, 2023[8]).

### Figure 2.5. Lending from multilateral creditors was not sufficient to counterbalance negative private capital outflows in 2022

Net debt inflows to low and middle income countries, 2012-22

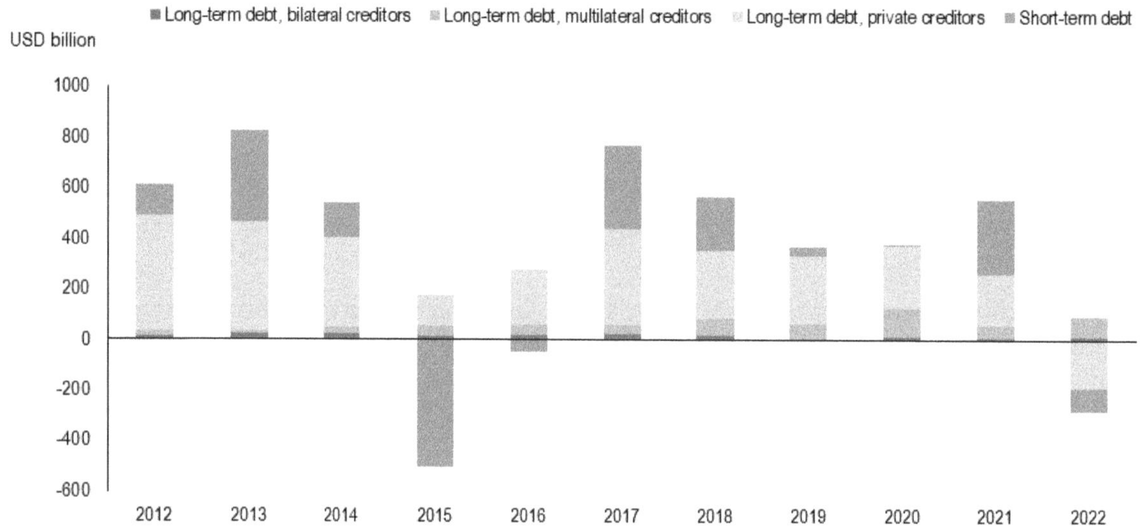


Note: Short-term debt includes all debt having an original maturity of one year or less and interest in arrears on long-term debt (such as treasury bills).
Source: World Bank Group (2024[9]), *International Debt Statistics* (database), https://www.worldbank.org/en/programs/debt-statistics/ids.

**As the global financing context evolves and developing countries face mounting challenges, there is a continuous need for multilateral institutions to adapt, improve and innovate.** The key role played by the multilateral development system in extending affordable financing to developing countries highlights its relevance, but also its need to keep improving. To continue playing an important role in the future, multilateral organisations must stay ahead of emerging issues and proactively look for ways to adapt their support to countries' evolving needs. Section 2.2. delves into the ongoing evolution of the MDBs as part of broader efforts to reform the global financial architecture. It explores how MDBs are being reshaped to better serve the needs of developing countries in a rapidly changing world. Meanwhile, Section 2.3. focuses on the need to look beyond the ongoing MDB reform to achieve a coherent and well-balanced multilateral development architecture. By pursuing these concurrent agendas, the multilateral development system can continue to play a pivotal role in global development, ensuring that multilateral organisations remain relevant and effective in addressing present and future development challenges.

## New global challenges call for multilateral development finance to expand its focus and capabilities

### *The multilateral development system is at the forefront of efforts to reform the global financial architecture*

**The widening gap between countries' aspirations and their financial resources has sparked calls to reform the global financial architecture.** Since 2021, multiple calls for reform have drawn attention to the need to scale up multilateral development finance and revisit the toolkit and operational model of the major international financial institutions, namely the International Monetary Fund (IMF) and the main MDBs (US Department of State, 2022[10]; Government of Barbados, 2022[11]). These calls underscore the need for a system better equipped to handle a growing number of development challenges in a context of multiple overlapping crises.

**The success or failure of current efforts to reform the global financial architecture hinge in large part on the multilateral development system.** Multilateral organisations are integral to the global financial architecture, providing essential financing, technical expertise and global knowledge. While the last major reform of the global financial architecture, in the aftermath of the 2009-2010 global financial crisis, focused on enhancing global governance to ensure macroeconomic and financial stability, the current reform drive aims to scale up and realign global efforts towards achieving the sustainable development agenda.

**The current reform drive is part of a broader, dynamic process of continuous improvement within the multilateral development system.** Since its inception, the multilateral development system has continuously evolved through the expansion of its architecture and the implementation of multilateral reform processes, many of which are still ongoing. Figure 2.6 illustrates some of the major reforms that have occurred within the multilateral development system since 2015. These include the creation of new multilateral entities such as the Asian Infrastructure Investment Bank (AIIB), the New Development Bank (NDB) and the Green Climate Fund (GCF). Additionally, significant agreements and processes have been implemented to enhance the policies and practices of multilateral stakeholders. This includes the 2016 Grand Bargain, which aims to enhance the funding of humanitarian activities, and the UNDS reform[1] launched in 2018 (Inter-Agency Standing Committee, 2024[12]; United Nations, 2024[13]). However, specific components of these reforms aimed at improving the way multilateral organisations are funded, such as the recently updated UN Funding Compact, have so far shown mixed progress (United Nations, 2024[13]).

## Figure 2.6. The multilateral development system is continuously evolving

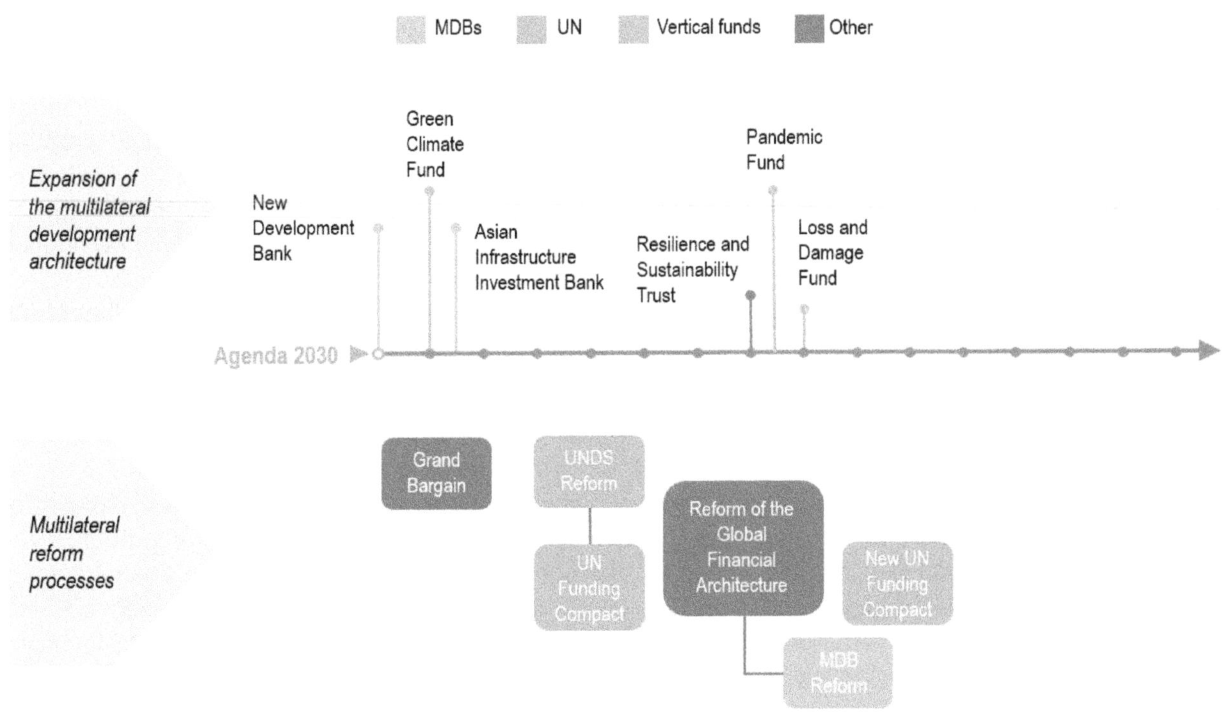


**The current push for MDB reforms, although unprecedented in scale and ambition, follows on from prior efforts to achieve greater efficiency.** Over the past decade, many MDBs have already made significant efforts to better leverage the resources entrusted to them. The G20 has steadily advocated for increased efficiency in the use of MDBs' capital resources, including through the MDB Action Plan on

Balance Sheet Optimisation approved in 2015 (G20, 2015[14]). The efforts undertaken include the mergers of MDBs' windows, the introduction of hybrid funding models or risk transfers. These innovations have enabled MDBs to steadily increase the volume of financing commitments from their concessional windows, even though donor contributions remained flat (OECD, 2022[3]). These actions underscore that the MDB system is a dynamic and adaptive force in development finance. They also reflect the strong emphasis of previous and ongoing reforms on financial innovation as the engine of MDBs' growth, leading to a growing financialisation of the multilateral development system. This financialisation refers to the increasing reliance on new financial instruments and financial innovations to expand the system's financial capacity – a topic further discussed in Chapter 3.

**As part of the current drive to reform the global financial architecture, the main international financial institutions have been asked by their shareholders and members to undergo a triple transformation.** Current reforms are largely focused on strengthening the financing capacity of the system. They place high expectations on MDBs and aims to equip them to better meet 21st century challenges. The triple transformation encompasses changes in their mandates, operational models and toolbox:

1. **The evolution of mandates** involves expanding beyond their traditional focus on poverty and inequality to also address global challenges.
2. **The shift in operational model** aims to improve the ways these institutions work, including by transforming their country engagement, to ensure they deliver enhanced development outcomes.
3. **Transforming the multilateral toolbox** involves leveraging financial innovation to increase MDBs' lending capacity and accelerate the mobilisation of private finance.

### *Despite gaining significant prominence, the MDB reform has experienced uneven progress*

**A change of scale in MDBs' capabilities is required to meet their expanded mandates.** A 2023 report on MDB reform by the G20 Independent Expert Group (IEG) highlighted the need for a substantial increase in MDBs' financing capacity (G20 IEG, 2023[15]). The report suggested that MDBs should gradually increase their annual financing to reach USD 260 billion by 2030, effectively tripling their 2019 financing volume from approximately USD 130 billion to USD 390 billion annually. In addition, the report suggested that MDBs need to mobilise five times more private capital and recommended that they adopt new financial instruments and strategies to achieve these goals.

**Although reforms are still ongoing, recent estimates suggest that MDBs could potentially increase their lending capacity by up to 30%.** The World Bank Group's Evolution Roadmap, updated in September 2023, indicates that the institution could boost its lending capacity by USD 50 billion to USD 150 billion over the next decade, representing an annual average increase of USD 5 billion to USD 15 billion (Development Committee, 2023[16]). On the occasion of the 2024 World Bank-IMF Spring meetings, the heads of ten MDBs released a joint Viewpoint Note (African Development Bank et al., 2024[17]), which estimates that their institutions could collectively expand their lending headroom by an additional USD 300 billion to USD 400 billion over the coming ten years, equating to an annual average increase of USD 30 billion to USD 40 billion. Figure 2.7 lays out various scenarios based on these estimates. It illustrates that the current MDB reform could lead to up to a 30% increase in MDB financing, compared to their commitment levels of 2019.

**Figure 2.7. The current MDB reform drive could support a 30% increase in MDB financing**

Scenarios of annual MDB reform gains

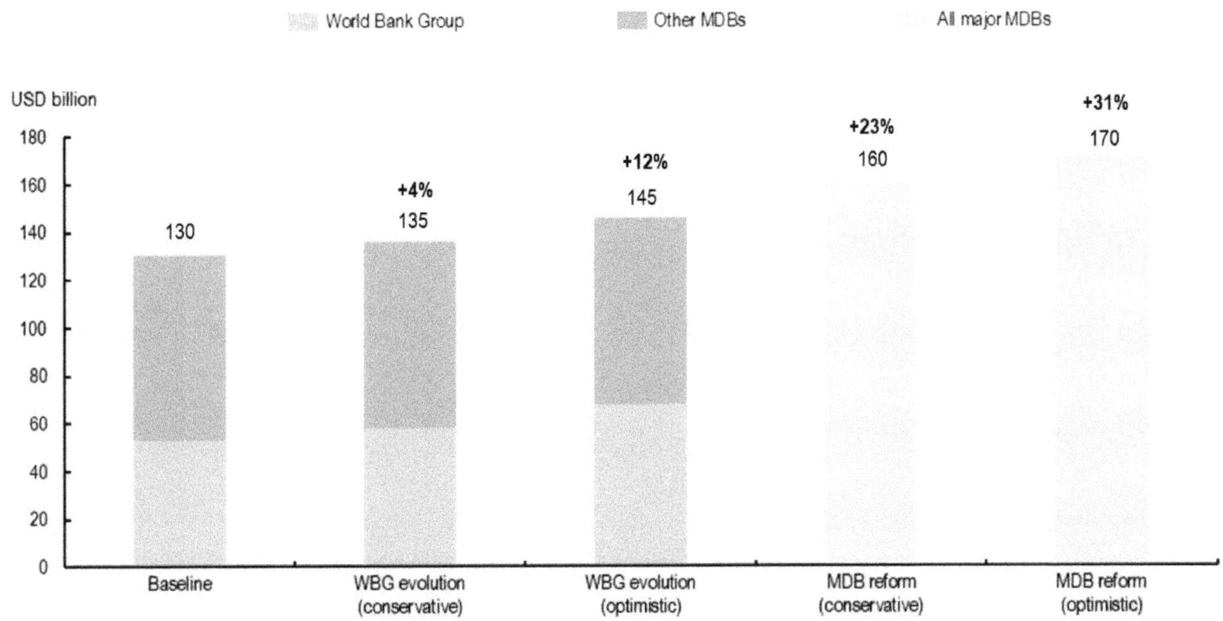


| Scenario | Description |
|---|---|
| **Baseline** | MDB commitments in 2019 |
| **WBG evolution (conservative)** | Measures from the WBG Evolution Roadmap endorsed at the 2023 Spring meetings |
| **WBG evolution (optimistic)** | All measures outlined in the WBG Evolution Roadmap |
| **MDB reform (conservative)** | Conservative estimate from the 2024 Viewpoint Note of the heads of major MDBs |
| **MDB reform (optimistic)** | Optimistic estimate from the 2024 Viewpoint Note of the heads of major MDBs |

Note: The ten major MDBs considered for this analysis include the World Bank Group (WBG), the African Development Bank, the Asian Development Bank, the Asian Infrastructure Investment Bank, the Council of Europe Development Bank, the European Bank for Reconstruction and Development, the European Investment Bank, the Inter-American Development Bank, the Islamic Development Bank and the New Development Bank.
Source: Authors' calculations based on information from Development Committee (2023[16]), *Ending Poverty on a Livable Planet: Report to Governors on World Bank Evolution*, https://www.devcommittee.org/content/dam/sites/devcommittee/doc/documents/2023/Final%20Updated%20Evolution%20Paper%20DC2023-0003.pdf and African Development Bank et al, (2024[17]), *MDBs Working as a System for Impact and Scale*, https://www.iadb.org/document.cfm?id=EZIDB0000577-986313001-135.

**While significant, these financial gains from current multilateral reforms fall short of initial expectations.** An analysis comparing current reform pathways with the G20 IEG target reveals a significant gap (Figure 2.8). Even under the optimistic scenario of USD 400 billion in additional lending capacity from MDB reforms over ten years, which corresponds to the upper range of the estimate provided in the joint MDB Viewpoint Note, this translates into an average of USD 40 billion per year (Figure 2.7) – substantially less than the additional USD 260 billion per year targeted by the G20 IEG. By 2030, this discrepancy could amount to a cumulative financing shortfall of around USD 755 billion. Bridging this substantial gap would require exploring additional options beyond the balance sheet optimisation measures and financial innovations currently under consideration. Among other things, this could involve ensuring successful replenishments of MDBs' concessional windows and securing capital increases from these institutions' shareholders.

**Figure 2.8. The estimates of additional lending capacity from the MDB reform remains far from initial expectations**

MDB commitments (2006-22) and pathways for scaling MDB financing capacity (2022-32)

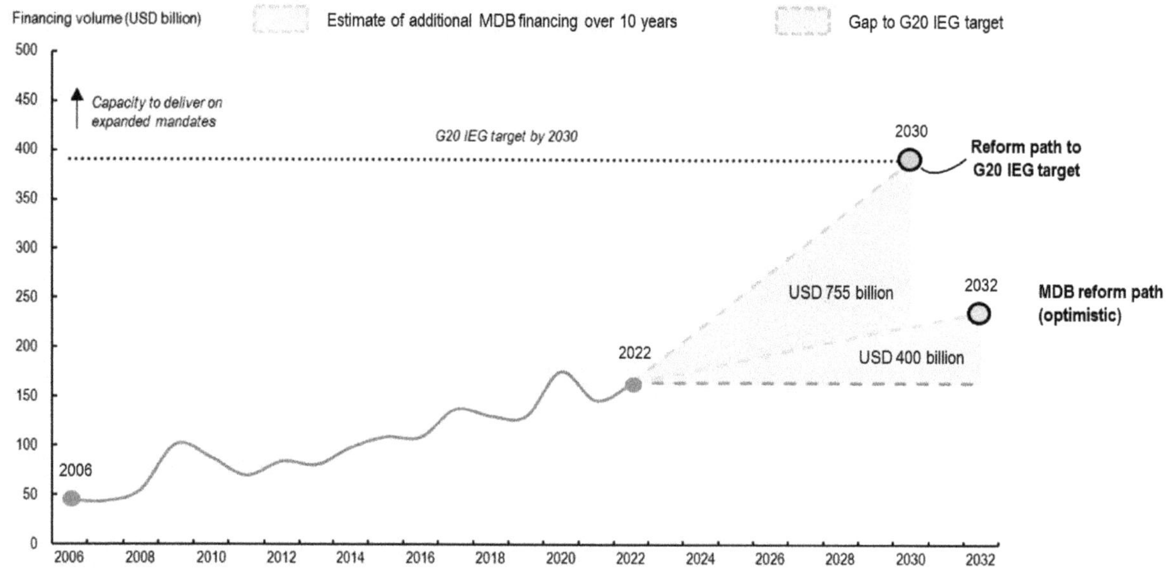


Source: Authors' calculations based on OECD (2024[2]), OECD Data Explorer, *Creditor Reporting System* (database), http://data-explorer.oecd.org/s/c and information from African Development Bank et al. (2024[17]), *MDBs Working as a System for Impact and Scale*, https://www.iadb.org/document.cfm?id=EZIDB0000577-986313001-135.

**Following three years of ambitious discussions on MDB reforms, tangible impacts on sustainable development have yet to materialise.** The slow progress is understandable given the complexity and technicality of the proposed reforms, their political implications, and the challenging geopolitical context. Nonetheless, these global discussions have at least facilitated a notable convergence among the main MDBs around a shared reform agenda. All MDBs are making efforts to implement various components of this agenda, indicating a collective commitment to advancing these critical reforms despite the inherent challenges.

**Progress has been uneven across reform areas.** Recent research has tracked the progress made by MDBs across five reform areas to operationalise the triple transformation (Center for Global Development, 2024[18]). This includes expanding MDBs' mandates beyond their traditional focus on poverty reduction to include global challenges, such as climate action and pandemic prevention (evolution of mandates); adding and making more efficient use of shareholders' capital, including by increasing private finance mobilisation (transforming the multilateral toolbox); and strengthening country engagement and operational efficiency (shift in operational model). As summarised in Table 2.1, the most significant and consistent progress has been made in expanding MDBs' mandates. Nearly all major MDBs (86%) have made considerable strides in incorporating global challenges into their mission statements. Other aspects of the reform agenda are advancing more slowly and have shown mixed or insufficient results. For instance, efforts to increase the mobilisation of private finance and to use capital more efficiently have respectively seen significant progress in only 57% and 47% of the main MDBs. Furthermore, progress has been notably insufficient in two crucial reform areas. Efforts to strengthen engagement with countries have only seen significant progress in 45% of MDBs, while attempts to increase their capital have lagged, with just 39% making headway.

**Table 2.1. There are large differences in implementation rate across MDBs and MDB reform areas**

| Areas of MDB reform | Percentage of MDBs that have made significant progress | Action showing the most progress (% of MDBs that have made significant progress) | Action showing the least progress (% of MDBs that have made significant progress) |
|---|---|---|---|
| **1. Making more efficient use of capital** | 47% | Free up capital through donor guarantees at the portfolio level (86%) | Appropriately value callable capital (29%) |
| **2. Adding to capital** | 39% | Undertake regular capital reviews based on standardised metrics (57%) | Pursue capital increases (29%) |
| **3. Expand mandates to include global challenges** | 86% | Incorporate global challenges into institutional mandates (100%) | Integrate global challenges into the majority of country diagnostics and strategies (71%) |
| **4. Transform engagement with countries** | 45% | Engage through country platforms (86%) | Deploy sovereign guarantees as a significant share of commitments (0%) |
| **5. Increase mobilisation of private finance** | 57% | Deploy subordinated products (e.g., guarantees, equity, and subordinated debt) as a significant share of non-sovereign commitments (100%) | Set and publish targets for private capital mobilisation (43%) |

Note: "Significant progress" means that MDBs have already implemented, or started implementing, relevant actions. The analysis covers seven of the largest MDBs: African Development Bank, Asian Development Bank, Asian Infrastructure Investment Bank, European Bank for Reconstruction and Development, European Investment Bank Global, Inter-American Development Bank Group, and World Bank Group.
Source: Center for Global Development (2024[18]), *Multilateral Development Bank Reform Tracker*, https://www.cgdev.org/page/mdb-reform-tracker.

**Progress on various reform areas is also uneven across the MDBs.** The variations in progress and focus across MDBs reflect their different characteristics and comparative advantages, but also suggest an opportunity for these institutions to share knowledge and experiences. For example, the African Development Bank (AfDB) already meets several of the requirements of the current MDB reform agenda to enhance MDBs' country engagement. These include targets to improve operational efficiency and shorten its project approval process. Another example is provided by the European Bank for Reconstruction and Development (EBRD), which has achieved notable results in mobilising private finance. Unlike many other MDBs, the EBRD has established targets for private capital mobilisation and makes extensive use of subordinated instruments (guarantees, equity, subordinated debt) as part of its portfolio. These examples illustrate that while progress may vary, there are valuable lessons and strategies within individual MDBs that could benefit the broader system.

**Beyond the current emphasis on MDB reform, it is crucial to ensure that the broader multilateral development system works coherently and effectively.** The MDB focus of ongoing reforms should not distract from the need to strengthen the other parts of the multilateral development system and to continue to pursue unfinished reforms, such as the UNDS reform. A well-balanced and effectively governed multilateral development system is vital for the success of global reform efforts and for providing the necessary support to developing countries as they strive to achieve their sustainable development goals. Section 2.3 shows that the continued expansion of the multilateral development architecture has introduced some vulnerabilities and challenges in the system, which, if left unaddressed, could undermine its capacity to deliver.

## A coherent and well-balanced architecture is crucial for successful multilateral reform

**While the emphasis of current reforms on expanding the mandates and capacity of MDBs is positive, the resulting increase in complexity needs to be managed.** MDBs play a crucial role in financing sustainable development, and enhancing their operational capabilities can significantly boost progress. However, it is equally important to address the vulnerabilities that emerge as the multilateral development system expands and evolves. In particular, this expansion has led to increased complexity and fragmentation over time, as examined in this section. Moreover, the pivotal roles of other parts of this system, including entities with important normative functions, must not be overlooked. Previous editions of this report have also examined the reform processes undertaken by other components of the multilateral development system, including the UNDS, highlighting recent and ongoing efforts and remaining challenges to enhancing its effectiveness (OECD, 2022[3]; OECD, 2020[1]). This systemic perspective is crucial to ensure that the multilateral development system can address the multifaceted issues facing developing countries effectively.

### *Multilateral growth and innovation have increased the complexity of the system's architecture*

**The growth of multilateral development finance in response to new development challenges has been accompanied by an expansion of the multilateral architecture.** The number of entities listed in the list of ODA-eligible international organisations has risen from 121 in 2000 to 212 in 2020 (Figure 2.9). This constant expansion reflects a tendency among stakeholders of the multilateral development system to establish new entities in response to each new crisis or development challenge.

Figure 2.9. The multilateral architecture is comprised of a growing number of entities

Number of ODA-eligible international organisations, 2010-22

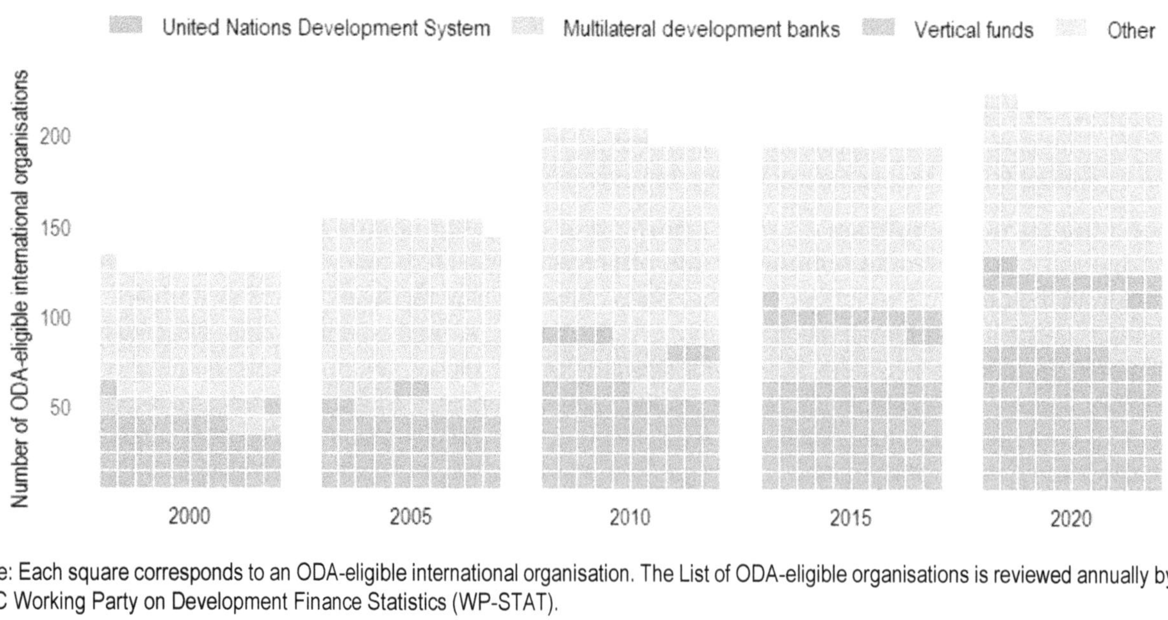


Note: Each square corresponds to an ODA-eligible international organisation. The List of ODA-eligible organisations is reviewed annually by the DAC Working Party on Development Finance Statistics (WP-STAT).

Source: Historical records of the list of ODA-eligible international organisations (OECD, not published).

**The existence of numerous multilateral organisations is not inherently negative and can be preferable to a proliferation of individual bilateral initiatives.** In fact, these international organisations are often established as vehicles to pool resources and tackle regional or global issues more effectively. For example, development partners' support to a vertical fund like Gavi, the Vaccine Alliance, often reflects their conviction that such collective initiatives will yield better development impact than pursuing the same goals through bilateral approaches.

**As new entities are created and existing ones broaden their mandates and operational capabilities, the multilateral development architecture becomes more versatile but also more intricate.** Over time, this expansion leads to a crowded and multi-layered architecture that can present significant challenges in terms of division of labour, co-ordination and overall effectiveness. Managing this growth effectively is essential for maintaining a coherent and robust multilateral system. However, this requires a proactive stance to identify areas that may be overcrowded or where the division of labour could be improved. Building consensus on solutions to streamline and optimise the system represents a significant challenge, demonstrated by the scarcity of instances in which the multilateral development architecture has been rationalised. A notable exception is the successful merger of four entities into UN Women in 2010, which underscored both the feasibility and complexity of such restructuring efforts. In addition, the growing complexity of the multilateral development system also requires co-ordination to ensure multilateral organisations are better able to help deliver on the ambitious global development agenda (Box 2.2).

**Over time, the creation of new multilateral organisations has contributed to donor proliferation at the country level.** Donor proliferation is a significant issue within the entire development co-operation landscape, not just within the multilateral development system. In fact, research suggests that this proliferation may be even more pronounced in bilateral development co-operation (World Bank Group, 2022[19]). However, the multilateral sphere is increasingly affected as well. Between 2010 and 2022, the number of multilateral donors active in each country has risen substantially. Whereas the majority of developing countries hosted 16 to 20 multilateral donors between 2010 and 2022, this number increased to between 26 to 30 donors per country from 2020 to 2022 (Figure 2.10). And while no country hosted more than 25 multilateral donors in 2010-2012, 82 countries had surpassed this threshold by 2020-2022. Research has shown that growing donor proliferation can complicate co-ordination, hamper country ownership and strain the administrative capacities of recipient countries, underscoring the need to strive for greater systemic coherence (World Bank Group, 2022[19]).

**Figure 2.10. The number of multilateral donors in ODA-eligible countries has increased substantially over the past decade**

Number of multilateral donors per ODA-eligible country, 2010-12 versus 2020-22

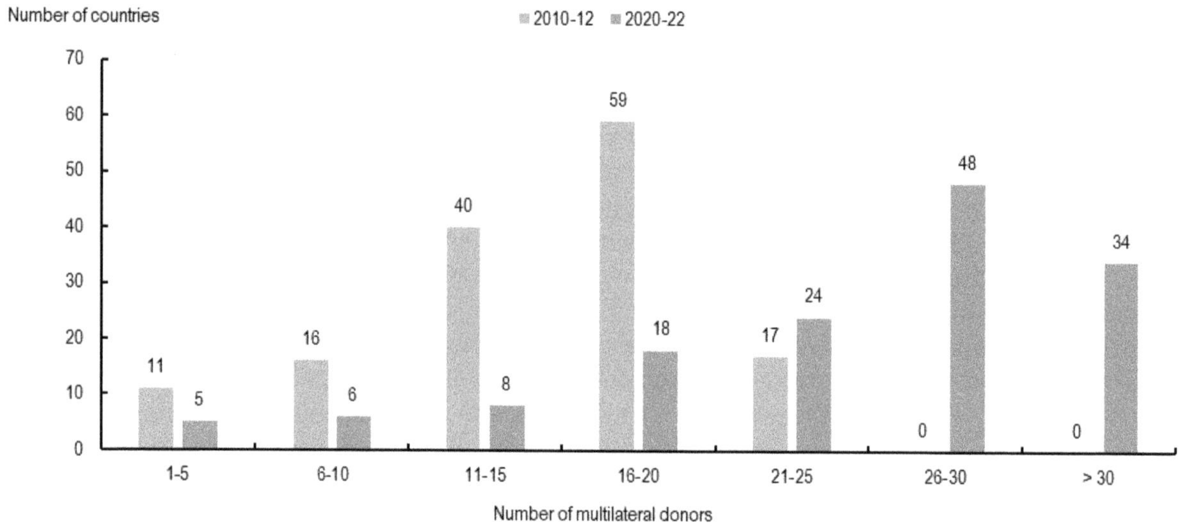


Source: Authors' calculations, based on OECD (2024[2]), OECD Data Explorer, *Creditor Reporting System* (database), http://data-explorer.oecd.org/s/c, adapted from World Bank Group (2022[19]), *Understanding Trends in Donor Proliferation and Fragmentation for Aid Effectiveness During Crises*, https://thedocs.worldbank.org/en/doc/ef73fb3d1d33e3bf0e2c23bdf49b4907-0060012022/understanding-trends-in-proliferation-and-fragmentation-for-aid-effectiveness-during-crises.

**The challenge is that as most funding is allocated at the country level, many multilateral organisations seek a presence in country.** Even multilateral organisations with a mandate to primarily conduct normative work at the global level have set up country offices. Examples include the United Nations Environment Program (UNEP) and the United Nations Human Settlements Programme (UN Habitat). Establishing new country-level structures incurs significant transaction costs for donors and recipients. Instead, multilateral stakeholders should explore whether and how one entity could represent others or handle implementation. While since 2018 the UN system has been taking steps through the UNDS reform to increase co-ordination, mainstreaming such approaches would ultimately necessitate a change in how member states fund UNDS entities, to encourage more integrated and efficient use of resources, thereby reducing transaction costs and maximising impact at the country level.

### Box 2.2. The need for multilateral collaboration at multiple levels for system-wide impact

**Recent assessments by the Multilateral Organisation Performance Assessment Network (MOPAN) have highlighted the need for the multilateral development system to work more holistically to help achieve common goals.** While a healthy dose of competition in the multilateral system can foster innovation, continued fragmentation may lead to incoherence, gaps and duplication, particularly at the country level.

**A coherent approach to collaboration is often lacking within multilateral organisations or sectors.** MOPAN's recent World Bank assessment identified challenges for MDBs in engaging in strategic, systematic and results-based partnerships rather than ad-hoc approaches (MOPAN, 2023[20]). In contrast, the assessment of the World Bank Group's private arm, IFC, revealed that its operated its partnerships in a structured manner around key strategic issues (MOPAN, 2021[21]). While MDBs are increasingly identifying new platforms for partnerships as part of their ongoing evolution, they remain more likely to compete than collaborate. When trade-offs need to be made, investment activities are given priority over co-ordination because the latter is currently not resourced, measured or incentivised. There also remains important challenges in coordination between the MDBs, the IMF and the UN.

**To support collaboration, it is key to see how organisations are structured internally.** MOPAN's assessment of the International Fund for Agricultural Development (IFAD) shows how it has improved its collaboration with national governments and development partners through increased decentralisation of staff posts and decision-making (MOPAN, 2024[22]). This has improved the relevance of its interventions and their alignment with community needs and national government strategies. Improved collaboration and strategic engagement with other Rome-based agencies has also helped. Other MDBs need to co-ordinate better internally, particularly for creating an enabling environment for private sector mobilisation, which has been a key feature of MDB reforms.

**Partnership-based operating models are conducive to collaboration.** MOPAN's forthcoming assessment of Gavi highlights how the structure of the alliance and its engagement with external partners allows it to benefit from their complementary skills and areas of expertise. It also supports agility, efficiency and effectiveness as well as synergies and common standards. The Global Partnership for Education's (GPE) diverse constituency-based board, is another example, playing an important role in strengthening collaboration in the increasingly complex and crowded global architecture for education. In addition, GPE's participation in the SDG4 Education 2030 High-Level Steering Committee (HLSC) helps reinforce collaboration at a global level by providing a forum to optimise roles and responsibilities.

**Collaboration also relies on incentives from system-level reforms.** MOPAN's current assessment of UN-Habitat shows how it has helped smaller UN entities to increase their contribution at the country level via the UN Sustainable Development Cooperation Frameworks. UN-Habitat also strengthened inter-agency collaboration through ten new memorandums of understanding (MoUs) with other UN entities since 2018.

**Multilateral organisations also need to work closely as a system to respond to the complex, multi-dimensional challenges inherent in crisis contexts.** MOPAN's recent assessments of IOM, UNHCR and WFP show that these organisations are making efforts to strengthen co-ordination, clarify roles, and enable joined-up country planning and resourcing (MOPAN, 2024[23]; MOPAN, 2022[24]). However, a report on the implementation of the humanitarian-development-peace nexus points to more work required to strengthen system-wide coherence and learning, as well as complementarity between humanitarian assistance, development co-operation and peace efforts in crisis contexts (OECD, 2022[25]).

Note: The assessments cited in this box can be found on MOPAN's website (MOPAN, 2024[26]), https://www.mopanonline.org/.

### *The expansion of the multilateral architecture contributes to fragmentation*

**The fragmentation of the multilateral architecture poses a significant challenge to aid effectiveness.** The multilateral development system reflects the broader development co-operation landscape, marked by geopolitical polarisation and reduced trust, resulting in more fragmented and piecemeal approaches. This means that development efforts are scattered across numerous initiatives, often resulting in diminished impact and increased transaction costs. As a result, aligning support with the priorities of recipient countries becomes more difficult, undermining country ownership and the effectiveness of development interventions.

**Efforts to mitigate aid fragmentation were prominent in international agreements at the beginning of the century but have not yielded tangible results.** Development partners and developing countries pledged to reduce fragmentation through commitments made in the Paris Declaration in 2005, the Accra Agenda for Action in 2008 and the Busan Declaration in 2011 (OECD, 2011[27]; OECD, 2008[28]; OECD, 2005[29]). Research indicates that despite the efforts outlined in these international agreements, there has been a significant increase in fragmentation since the early 1970s. Notably, there has been no observed reduction in fragmentation following the Paris Declaration (Gehring et al., 2017[30]). Going forward, such agreements are unlikely to yield results without understanding the underlying reasons for the continued proliferation of multilateral initiatives.

**Fragmentation can lead to a proliferation of smaller projects, spreading resources across an increasing number of activities, sectors and recipients.** For instance, while the average MDB project size increased by 52% between 2010 and 2022 (Figure 2.11), the average project size of vertical funds decreased by 30% while UNDS projects saw a slight decrease (of 6%). This variation highlights that the various components of the multilateral development system experience and manage fragmentation differently, reflecting their unique operational contexts and mandates. Understanding these differences is crucial for devising targeted strategies to address fragmentation and ensure that development aid remains effective and impactful.

## Figure 2.11. The average project size in vertical funds and UN entities has decreased

Average project size by type of multilateral organisation, 2010-12 versus 2020-22

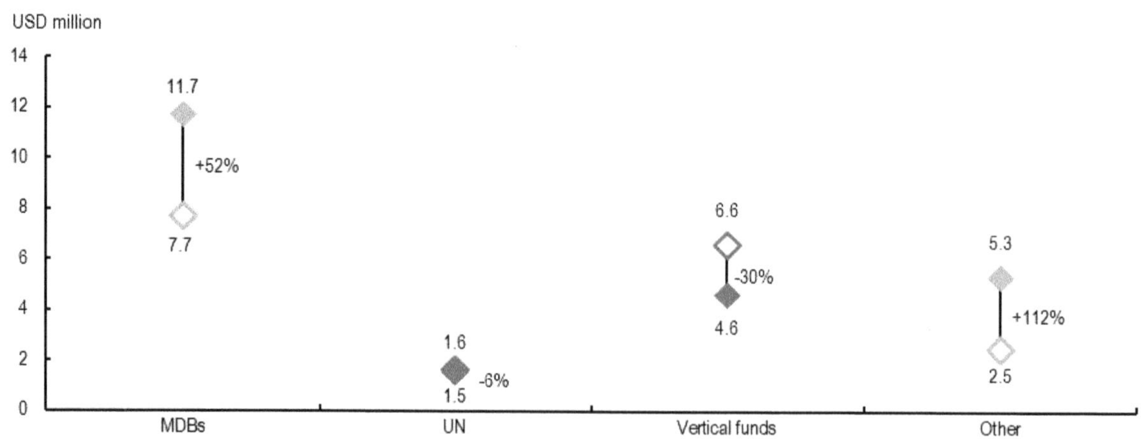


Note: The colours indicate whether the change in average project size is positive (green) or negative (red).
Source: Authors' calculations, based on OECD (2024[2]), OECD Data Explorer, *Creditor Reporting System* (database), http://data-explorer.oecd.org/s/c.

**A well-balanced and effectively governed multilateral development system requires complementing efficiency with effectiveness and adopting a system-wide perspective.** This involves considering the role of all multilateral actors and addressing often-neglected or unfinished areas of reform, such as system-wide coherence, co-ordination, transparency and accountability. These factors are gaining importance as the system's constant growth introduces vulnerabilities that need to be balanced with architecture and systemic improvements, as well as efforts to strengthen multilateral effectiveness. To support this effort, it is important to generate evidence for the quality aspects of multilateral development co-operation. This is the role of initiatives such as the Global Partnership for Effective Development Co-operation (GPEDC) monitoring exercise (Box 2.3).

### Box 2.3. How the GPEDC monitoring exercise contributes to transparency, dialogue, trust and accountability

**The monitoring exercise of the Global Partnership for Effective Development Co-operation (GPEDC) generates evidence to assess the quality of development co-operation** and partnerships for development, including for bilateral and multilateral development partners. The exercise also provides evidence to follow-up on the implementation of the UN Funding Compact.

**By engaging in the monitoring exercise and participating in country-level data collection, multilateral organisations can benchmark their performance** on the implementation of the internationally agreed effectiveness principles. Evidence is generated across four dimensions: (1) whole of society approach to development: assesses whether multilateral organisations engage a diversity of country-level stakeholder groups in the development process and the quality of private sector engagement in development co-operation; (2) use of country systems: evaluates how multilateral organisations align with and use partner countries' core systems for development co-operation; (3) transparency: explores public availability of information on development co-operation; and (4) leaving no one behind: assesses how multilateral organisations ensure that everyone, including the vulnerable and marginalised, is consulted in development co-operation efforts.

**Results provide multilateral organisations with valuable insights into their strengths and weaknesses**, enabling them and their shareholders to allocate funding and resources more effectively. The results also contribute to transparency, dialogue and trust among stakeholders, and foster accountability in the multilateral development system.

**Results for Burkina Faso and Bosnia and Herzegovina** from the 2023-2026 round of the Global Partnership monitoring exercise offer early examples of how multilateral organisations are performing in these specific contexts.[2] The 2023-2026 round of the Global Partnership monitoring is taking place on a rolling basis, with countries undertaking the exercise at different times based on their preference and context. In both Burkina Faso and Bosnia and Herzegovina, multilateral organisations outperformed bilateral partners on average across multiple metrics of the monitoring framework:

- **Whole-of-society approach:** multilateral organisations engaged a broader range of country-level stakeholders in developing their country-level strategies than bilateral partners – including government, civil society organisations (CSOs), and private sector representatives. In Burkina Faso, multilateral organisations reported slightly higher inclusiveness of dialogues related to private sector engagement (PSE) in development co-operation than their bilateral counterparts. Additionally, a greater proportion of multilateral organisations track and share the results of PSE in development co-operation projects and programmes publicly. They also have more PSE-related grievance processes or mechanisms in place than bilateral partners.

- **Use of country systems:** multilateral organisations show greater alignment with partner country results frameworks and planning tools than bilateral partners. In line with overall results from the 2018 round, in both countries multilateral organisations considerably outperformed bilateral partners in using government data and statistics to track progress on implementing their country-level interventions. However, results are mixed for the use of Public Financial Management (PFM) systems when channelling development co-operation to the public sector. In Burkina Faso, multilateral organisations used PFM systems more frequently than bilateral partners, whereas in Bosnia and Herzegovina, they used PFM systems much less than bilateral partners.
- **Transparency:** in Burkina Faso, multilateral organisations lag behind bilateral partners in reporting to country-level information management systems for development co-operation and in sharing forward spending plans with the government (covering the next one to three years). The proportion of multilateral partners who make their country-level strategies publicly available is also significantly lower than for bilateral partners. This indicates a substantial opportunity to improve information sharing and transparency at the country level.
- **Leaving no one behind:** multilateral organisations also performed better on consulting women and girls, youth and children and vulnerable and marginalised groups of the population. Similarly to bilateral partners, multilateral organisations show a high degree of inclusion of development priorities for a diversity of population groups in their country-level strategies. This signals important steps towards meeting the pledge of leaving no one behind.

Source: Analysis by the Global Partnership for Effective Development Co-operation (GPEDC) based on information and data from the 2023-2026 GPEDC monitoring round, in particular the Burkina Faso Monitoring Results 2023-2026 (GPEDC, 2024[31]) and the Bosnia and Herzegovina Monitoring Results 2023-2026 (GPEDC, 2024[32]).

## Key chapter findings and recommendations

### *Key findings*

**The chapter has outlined the growing relevance of multilateral development finance in development co-operation, and highlights significant evolutions in the multilateral development architecture:**

- **Multilateral finance is assuming an increasingly central role in development co-operation**, as evidenced by the growing "market share" of the multilateral development system in total official development finance, from 45% to 61% between 2012 and 2022. In addition, OECD DAC members' total use of the multilateral development system has seen a gradual but steady increase over the past decade. From 37% in 2010, the share of funding channelled to or through multilateral organisations rose to 45% in 2021, before slightly declining to 43% in 2022. In the current high-risk post-pandemic context, characterised by a complex global financial environment with rising debt and high capital costs, multilateral institutions also play a crucial role in mobilising resources to help countries maintain financial stability.
- **There is a pressing need to expand the focus and capabilities of multilateral development finance in response to new global challenges.** Recent calls to reform multilateral development finance seek to triple MDBs' financing capacity and substantially scale up the mobilisation of private finance by 2030. These reforms highlight the need to adapt MDBs' mandates, operational models, and financial tools to tackle contemporary issues, such as climate change and pandemics, effectively. While significant progress has been made in expanding MDBs' mandates, other areas

such as private finance mobilisation and capital utilisation require further attention and improvement to meet the ambitious targets set out.

- **For multilateral reform efforts to deliver on their promises, it is crucial to maintain a coherent and well-balanced multilateral development architecture.** The system must evolve in a way that avoids the pitfalls of increased complexity and fragmentation, ensuring that all parts of the system work in harmony. Effective management of this growth, alongside a focus on enhancing coordination and reducing transaction costs, is essential. The analysis in this chapter underscores the importance of a systemic perspective in which reforms are not limited to MDBs but also consider the roles of other multilateral entities and the need for system-wide co-ordination. Ensuring a balance between efficiency and effectiveness will allow the multilateral development system to respond effectively to current and future global challenges.

### *Key recommendations:*

- **Prioritise the rationalisation of the multilateral architecture in global discussions:** Make systemic issues related to the expansion and fragmentation of the multilateral architecture a key agenda item in global fora, such as the FfD4 Conference and G20 meetings. Engage the heads of major IFIs, UN agencies, multilateral funds, and key official providers (e.g. G20 members) in this effort to provide guidance an co-ordinate actions according to their respective mandates. Promote and support global initiatives aimed at rationalising the multilateral architecture, especially in crowded sectors such as multilateral climate finance.
- **Promote greater collaboration in multilateral reforms:** Ensure a collaborative approach to MDB and UN reforms. Use existing fora to share experiences and lessons from individual organisations engaged in reform processes to benefit the broader system and avoid a siloed approach to multilateral reforms. Opportunities for MDB learning include the AfDB's transformation of country engagement, as well as EBRD's experience in private finance mobilisation. Similarly, ensure that UNDS entities learn from the successes and challenges of ongoing special agency reforms, such as WHO's.
- **Ensure coherence in multilateral development co-operation through whole-of-government approaches:** Strengthen dialogue among government functions (aid agencies, treasuries, ministries of foreign affairs) on cross-cutting multilateral issues, such as the MDB reform. This can ensure coherence and balance between financial considerations promoted by treasuries and the focus on development impact central to foreign relations and aid agencies' missions.
- **Harmonise donor requirements:** Address the lack of standardisation in bilateral and multilateral donor requirements to reduce the burden on multilateral organisations and recipient countries:
    - Use discussions at the governing body of each organisation to agree on common reporting needs from bilateral donors. This is increasingly important given the growing role of emerging donors, which could otherwise impose additional burdens on multilateral organisations.
    - Ensure multilateral organisations and funds harmonise their requirements to reduce transaction costs in accessing multilateral funds for recipient countries and mitigate the impact of donor proliferation.
- **Bring effectiveness principles to scale:** With close to half of ODA channelled through the multilateral system, it is important that the effectiveness principles adopted by bilateral donors – country ownership, focus on results, inclusive partnerships, transparency and mutual accountability – are not lost in the new global financing architecture. Reinvigorate the dialogue among and between multilateral and bilateral providers to operationalise and monitor the implementation of these principles in multilateral development co-operation.

## References

African Development Bank et al. (2024), *MDBs Working as a System for Impact and Scale*, https://www.adb.org/sites/default/files/news-release/962971/Heads-of-MDBs-Viewpoint-Note.pdf. [17]

Center for Global Development (2024), *Multilateral Development Bank Reform Tracker*, https://www.cgdev.org/page/mdb-reform-tracker (accessed on 2024). [18]

DAC Working Party on Development Finance Statistics (2023), *Converged Statistical Reporting Directives for the Creditor Reporting System (CRS) and the Annual DAC Questionnaire*, https://one.oecd.org/document/DCD/DAC/STAT(2023)9/FINAL/en/pdf. [4]

Development Committee (2023), *Ending Poverty on a Livable Planet: Report to Governors on World Bank Evolution*, https://www.devcommittee.org/content/dam/sites/devcommittee/doc/documents/2023/Final%20Updated%20Evolution%20Paper%20DC2023-0003.pdf. [16]

Diwan, I. and V. Songwe (2024), *Developing Countries Need Debt Relief to Act on Climate Change by Ishac Diwan & Vera Songwe - Project Syndicate*, https://www.project-syndicate.org/commentary/developing-countries-need-fiscal-space-for-investment-in-green-growth-by-ishac-diwan-and-vera-songwe-2024-01 (accessed on 3 June 2024). [7]

G20 (2015), *Multilateral Development Banks' Action Plan To Optimize Balance Sheets*, http://g20.org.tr/wp-content/uploads/2015/11/Multilateral-Development-Banks-Action-Plan-to-Optimize-Balance-Sheets.pdf. [14]

G20 IEG (2023), *Strengthening Multilateral Development Banks: The Triple Agenda*, https://www.cgdev.org/sites/default/files/The_Triple_Agenda_G20-IEG_Report_Volume1_2023.pdf. [15]

Gehring, K. et al. (2017), "Aid Fragmentation and Effectiveness: What Do We Really Know?", *World Development*, Vol. 99, pp. 320-334, https://doi.org/10.1016/J.WORLDDEV.2017.05.019. [30]

Government of Barbados (2022), *The 2022 Bridgetown Initiative for the Reform of the Global Financial Architecture*, https://pmo.gov.bb/wp-content/uploads/2022/10/The-2022-Bridgetown-Initiative.pdf. [11]

GPEDC (2024), *Bosnia and Herzegovina Monitoring Results 2023-2026*, Global Partnership for Effective Development Co-operation, https://www.effectivecooperation.org/Bosnia-Herzegovina-Monitoring-Results-2023-2026. [32]

GPEDC (2024), *Burkina Faso Monitoring Results 2023-2026*, Global Partnership for Effective Development Co-operation, https://www.effectivecooperation.org/Burkina-Faso-Monitoring-Results-2023-2026. [31]

Inter-Agency Standing Committee (2024), *The Grand Bargain (Official website)*, https://interagencystandingcommittee.org/grand-bargain. [12]

MOPAN (2024), *MOPAN Online*, http://www.mopanonline.org (accessed on July 2024). [26]

MOPAN (2024), *Performance at a glance: Office of the United Nations High Commissioner for Refugees (UNHCR)*, Multilateral Organisation Performance Assessment Network, https://www.mopanonline.org/assessments/unhcr/MOPAN_2024_Performance_Glance.pdf. [23]

MOPAN (2024), *Performance at a glance: The International Fund for Agricultural Development (IFAD)*, Multilateral Organisation Performance Assessment Network, https://www.mopanonline.org/assessments/ifad2023/MOPAN_IFAD_PaG.pdf. [22]

MOPAN (2023), *Performance at a glance: the World Bank*, Multilateral Organisation Performance Assessment Network, https://www.mopanonline.org/assessments/worldbank2021/World%20Bank%20Performance%20at%20a%20Glance.pdf. [20]

MOPAN (2022), *Performance at a glance: International Organization for Migration (IOM)*, Multilateral Organisation Performance Assessment Network, https://www.mopanonline.org/assessments/iom2022/IOM%20Performance%20at%20a%20Glance.pdf. [24]

MOPAN (2021), *Performance at a glance: The International Finance Corporation (IFC)*, Multilateral Organisation Performance Assessment Network, https://www.mopanonline.org/assessments/ifc2021/IFC%20Performance%20at%20a%20Glance_2024.pdf. [21]

OECD (2024), *Annex 2 List of ODA-eligible international organisations*, https://www.oecd.org/dac/financing-sustainable-development/development-finance-standards/annex2.htm. [5]

OECD (2024), "Creditor Reporting System", http://data-explorer.oecd.org/s/c. [2]

OECD (2024), *OECD Data Explorer*, https://data-explorer.oecd.org/ (accessed on  July 2024). [6]

OECD (2022), *Multilateral Development Finance 2022*, OECD Publishing, Paris, https://doi.org/10.1787/9fea4cf2-en. [3]

OECD (2022), *The Humanitarian-Development-Peace Nexus Interim Progress Review*, OECD Publishing, Paris, https://doi.org/10.1787/2f620ca5-en. [25]

OECD (2020), *Multilateral Development Finance 2020*, OECD Publishing, Paris, https://doi.org/10.1787/e61fdf00-en. [1]

OECD (2011), *Busan Partnership for Effective Development Co-operation: Fourth High Level Forum on Aid Effectiveness, Busan, Republic of Korea, 29 November - 1 December 2011*, Best Practices in Development Co-operation, OECD Publishing, Paris, https://doi.org/10.1787/54de7baa-en. [27]

OECD (2008), *Accra Agenda for Action*, OECD Publishing, Paris, https://doi.org/10.1787/9789264098107-en. [28]

OECD (2005), *Paris Declaration on Aid Effectiveness*, OECD Publishing, Paris, https://doi.org/10.1787/9789264098084-en. [29]

United Nations (2024), *Funding Compact for the United Nations' Support to the Sustainable Development Goals*, https://unsdg.un.org/sites/default/files/2024-06/Funding%20compact_English.pdf. [13]

US Department of State (2022), *Remarks by Secretary of the Treasury Janet L. Yellen at the Center for Global Development*, https://home.treasury.gov/news/press-releases/jy0997. [10]

World Bank (2023), *International Debt Report 2023*, Washington, DC: World Bank, https://doi.org/10.1596/40670. [8]

World Bank Group (2024), *International Debt Statistics*, https://www.worldbank.org/en/programs/debt-statistics/ids (accessed on  May 2024). [9]

World Bank Group (2022), *Understanding Trends in Proliferation and Fragmentation for Aid Effectiveness During Crises*, https://thedocs.worldbank.org/en/doc/ef73fb3d1d33e3bf0e2c23bdf49b4907-0060012022/understanding-trends-in-proliferation-and-fragmentation-for-aid-effectiveness-during-crises. [19]

## Notes

[1] The UNDS Reform is an comprehensive change process, launched in 2018, with the aim to align UNDS capabilities, organisation, co-ordination mechanisms, skillsets, and resources with the needs of the 2030 Agenda.

[2] Results for Bosnia and Herzegovina are based on reporting from 17 multilateral organisations, including 13 UN agencies, 2 Multilateral Development Banks, the European Union Institutions and the Organisation for Security and Co-operation in Europe.  Results for Burkina Faso are based on reporting from 15 multilateral organisations, including 12 UN agencies, 2 Multilateral Development Banks and the European Union Institutions.

# 3 Funding to the multilateral development system

DAC members' use of the multilateral system has grown continuously over the past decade, reaching record levels in 2022. This growth was largely driven by crisis response, while funding for long-term development goals remained stagnant. In addition, recent crises have also accelerated the rise of earmarked funding at the expense of core contributions, essential for the system to operate sustainably and respond flexibly to global challenges. Although DAC members remain the primary funders, some emerging donors are increasingly asserting their influence through strategic contributions. Their growing involvement brings new resources and opportunities but also affects the donor base and priorities of the multilateral development system.

## The crisis-induced growth of multilateral development finance is exacerbating existing tensions in the system

### *Total use of the multilateral system reached a new record high in 2022, driven by support to Ukraine*

**In 2022, DAC members' total use of the multilateral system reached a new record high, totalling USD 98.5 billion.** This comprised USD 50.6 billion in core contributions (multilateral ODA), while earmarked contributions (also known as non-core or multi-bi aid; see Chapter 2), amounted to USD 48 billion. This marked the seventh consecutive annual increase in total use of the multilateral system, underlining its continued relevance in the global development landscape.

**This growth masks diverging trends, with core contributions decreasing in 2022 while earmarked contributions continued to rise.** After four years of nearly parallel movements in core and earmarked contributions (Figure 3.1, Panel A.), 2022 marked a clear divergence, with core contributions dipping by 6% while earmarked contributions surged by 42% (Figure 3.1, Panel B.). This decline in core contributions, the largest in a decade, followed the record high of USD 53.4 billion achieved in the previous year. Although this drop came after three years of consecutive increases and may be temporary, its occurrence alongside a sharp rise in earmarked contributions is a warning signal that requires close monitoring.

Figure 3.1. In 2022, a sharp rise in earmarking contrasted with a decline in core multilateral contributions

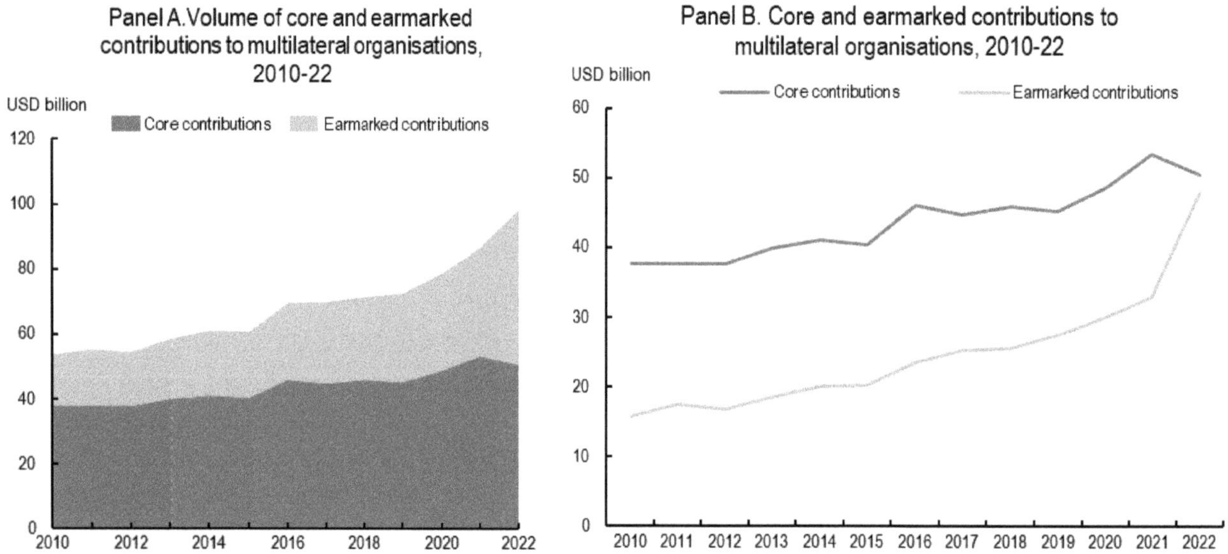


Note: The two graphs present DAC countries' total use of the multilateral development system, which covers both their core contributions (multilateral ODA) and their earmarked contributions (non-core, or multi-bi aid) to multilateral organisations. Calculations are based on disbursements, in 2022 constant prices.
Source: OECD (2024[1]), OECD Data Explorer, *Members' total use of the multilateral system* (database), http://data-explorer.oecd.org/s/s.

**The 2022 increase in total use of the multilateral development system can be attributed to a peak in support for Ukraine.** Several DAC members provided exceptional levels of support to Ukraine, primarily as budget support through the main international financial institutions (IFIs). This surge in support explains the significant rise in the share of earmarked contributions in total contributions observed in 2022. While earmarked contributions have gradually but steadily increased over the past decade, from 30% in 2010 to

38% in 2021, between 2021 and 2022 this share surged by 11 percentage points, from 38% to 49% (Figure 3.2).

### Figure 3.2. Recent crises have accelerated the use of earmarked contributions

Share of DAC countries' core and earmarked contributions to multilateral organisations, 2010-22

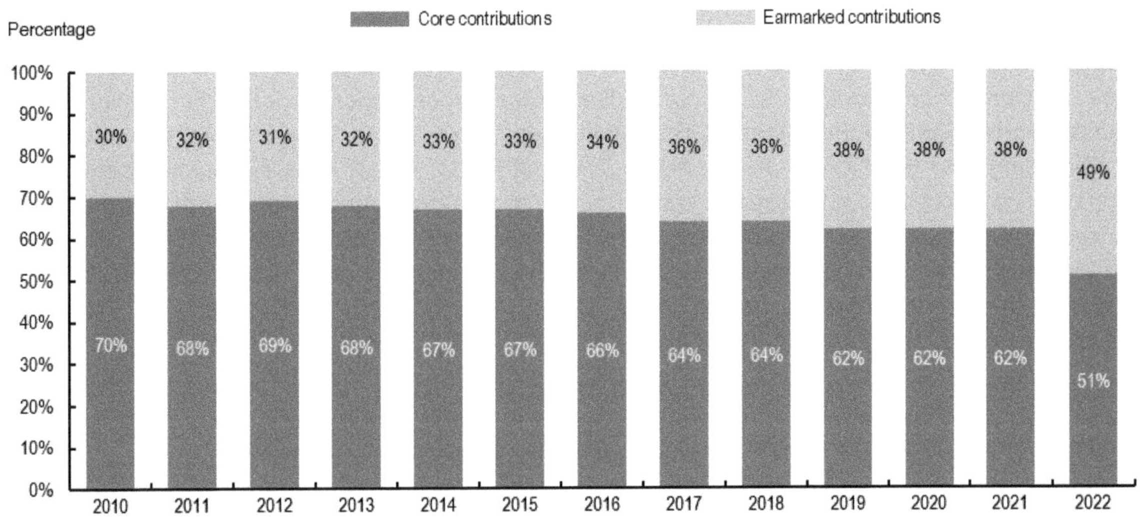


Note: The figure presents DAC countries' total use of the multilateral development system, which covers both their core contributions (multilateral ODA) and their earmarked contributions (non-core, or multi-bi aid) to multilateral organisations. Calculations are based on gross disbursements, in 2022 constant prices.
Source: OECD (2024[1]), OECD Data Explorer, *Members' total use of the multilateral system* (database), http://data-explorer.oecd.org/s/s.

### *Earmarked contributions are rising across the multilateral development system*

**The rise of earmarked contributions has been a persistent issue in parts of the multilateral development system.** Previous editions of this report showed that reliance on earmarked contributions varies across multilateral organisations, with the practice of earmarking being particularly prevalent within the UNDS (OECD, 2022[2]) (OECD, 2020[3]). This is partly due to the mandates of key UNDS entities, such as those involved in the delivery of humanitarian aid, which tend to receive a larger proportion of earmarked contributions. However, the growing imbalance between core and earmarked contributions across many UNDS entities cannot always be justified by their specific mandates or operational models, and also partly reflects broader issues related to stakeholders' incentives in a complex geopolitical context. Efforts to address this imbalance, including through the 2019 UN Funding Compact (United Nations, 2019[4]), have so far been unsuccessful.

**Although the UNDS' dysfunctional funding situation is widely acknowledged, multilateral stakeholders have insufficient incentives to change it.** Current trends in funding to the UNDS deviate significantly from the original funding model envisaged in the UN Charter, in which decisions in the General Assembly would determine the priorities and volume of budgets through mandatory assessed contributions by member states (OECD, 2015[5]). Recent research suggests that, in practice, earmarking is commonly used by donors to exert influence on multilateral organisations' priorities, bypassing the complex political negotiations associated with a change in core assessed contributions (Baumann and Haug, 2024[6]). According to the same research, UN managers themselves often prefer to avoid the lengthy and uncertain negotiations associated with assessed contributions, which are also prone to late payments. Additionally, some countries benefit from the status quo by paying less than their fair share of total UN income. However, despite these challenges, the research indicates that reform is possible, as illustrated by the World Health Organization's (WHO) ongoing efforts to rebalance the share of its core and earmarked contributions. This example demonstrates that while challenging, rebalancing funding models to reduce over-reliance on earmarked contributions is feasible with concerted effort and with commitment from all multilateral stakeholders.

**In recent years, successive crises have led to a widespread increase in earmarking across the rest of the multilateral development system.** This rise in earmarked contributions is no longer a UN-specific issue (Figure 1.4). In fact, recent surges in earmarked contributions cater to various motives and encompass diverse types of support and initiatives across the multilateral development system. For instance, earmarked contributions to the World Bank Group rose rapidly in 2022, largely as a means to channel support to Ukraine. For other MDBs, the largest increase in earmarked contributions occurred in 2020, coinciding with the COVID-19 pandemic. Vertical funds, which have historically been resourced through core contributions, also experienced a surge in non-core earmarked contributions from 2021, largely driven by increased funding earmarked through Gavi, the Vaccine Alliance. Lastly, earmarking to the IMF has surged as donors channel funds through the Poverty Reduction and Growth Trust (PRGT) to support countries impacted by successive crises.

## Figure 3.3. The rise of earmarking is no longer specific to the UN

DAC countries' core and earmarked contributions to multilateral organisations, 2010-22

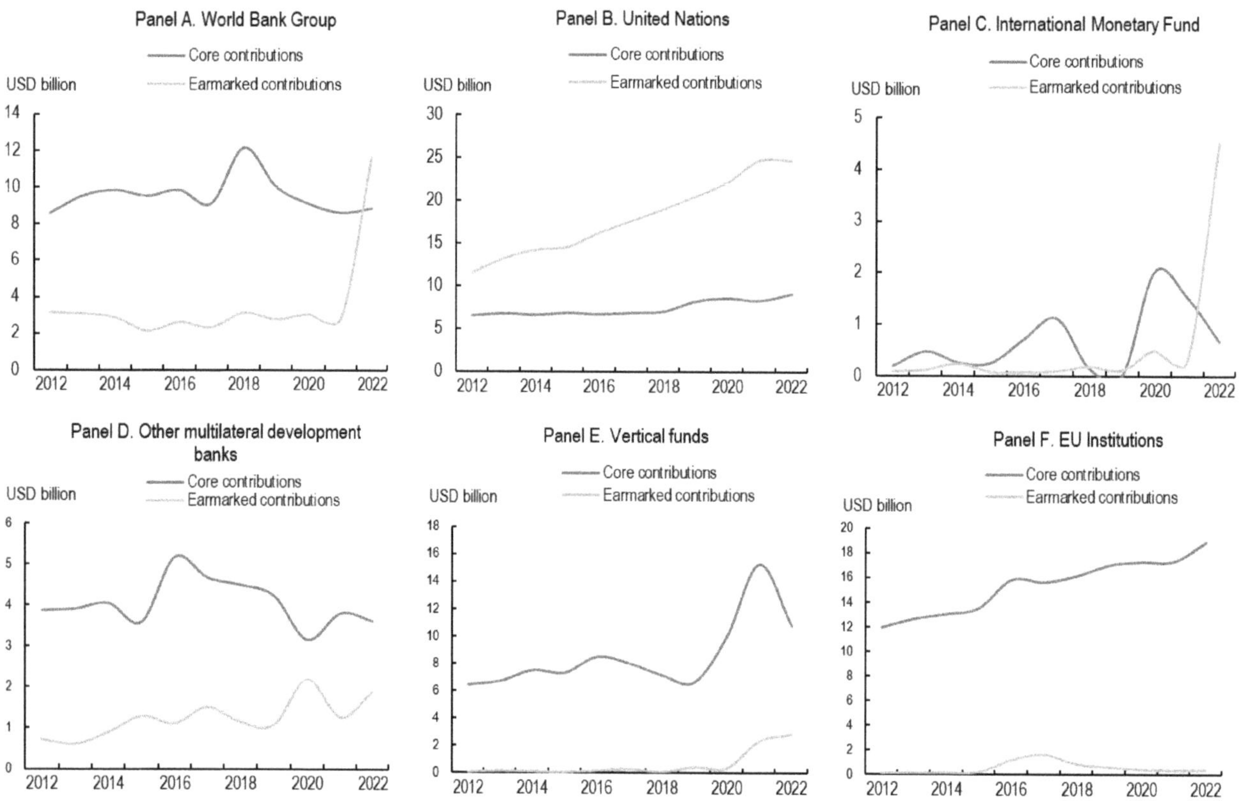


Note: The graphs present DAC countries' total use of the multilateral development system, which covers both their core contributions (multilateral ODA) and their earmarked contributions (non-core, or multi-bi aid) to multilateral organisations. Calculations are based on gross disbursements, in 2022 constant prices.
Source: OECD (2024[1]), OECD Data Explorer, *Members' total use of the multilateral system* (database), http://data-explorer.oecd.org/s/s.

**Addressing the rise of earmarking requires a nuanced approach that recognises both the challenges and the opportunities of this funding modality.** Recent research has shown that earmarked contributions are positively related to outcome performance – the extent to which multilateral organisations achieve results; but negatively related to process performance – the extent to which these organisations have rules and procedures in place to plan, manage their operations, liaise with partners and monitor results (Reinsberg and Siauwijaya, 2024[7]). Previous editions of this report have also highlighted both positive and negative effects of this funding modality (OECD, 2022[2]) (OECD, 2020[3]). On one hand, earmarked funding allows multilateral organisations to expand their activities beyond what would be possible with core funding alone. As shown in Section 3.1.3, it has for example been crucial in addressing recent crises and will in all certainty remain an important component of multilateral organisations' resource mix in the near to medium term. On the other hand, earmarking also presents several challenges. For individual organisations, these include funding vulnerability, since earmarked contributions tend to be less predictable, more volatile and more transaction-heavy than core contributions. It also leads to systemic issues explored in Section 2.2. In some cases, earmarking funds to multilateral agencies' crisis response plans can even undermine the very flexibility required in crisis and fragile situations, and can hinder the Resident Co-ordinator's role of driving greater co-ordination and prioritisation of development efforts across humanitarian, development and peace actors (Box 3.1). Ultimately, addressing the entrenchment and widespread use of earmarking across the multilateral development system will require strategies that acknowledge the variety of motives providers and multilateral organisations have for offering or accepting earmarked contributions, while promoting policies and practices that mitigate its disadvantages.

### *Growing multilateral contributions are driven by crisis response, rather than long-term sustainable development priorities*

**Contributions to the multilateral development system, excluding funds earmarked for recent crises, have remained relatively flat over the past decade.** Between 2012 and 2022, the increase in DAC countries' multilateral contributions was primarily driven by support earmarked for crisis response (Figure 1.5). In fact, multilateral contributions would have stagnated had it not been for crisis-response funding. Notably, contributions earmarked for humanitarian assistance, the response to the COVID-19 pandemic and Ukraine rose by more than 400% over the ten-year period, compared to a 43% increase in other multilateral contributions. This two-speed trend was also visible between 2021 and 2022, with contributions earmarked for crisis response surging by 49% while other contributions to the multilateral development system declined by 2%.

## Figure 3.4. Without crisis-response earmarking, multilateral contributions would have stagnated

DAC countries' core contributions and contributions earmarked for humanitarian, COVID-19, Ukraine and other development purposes, 2012-22

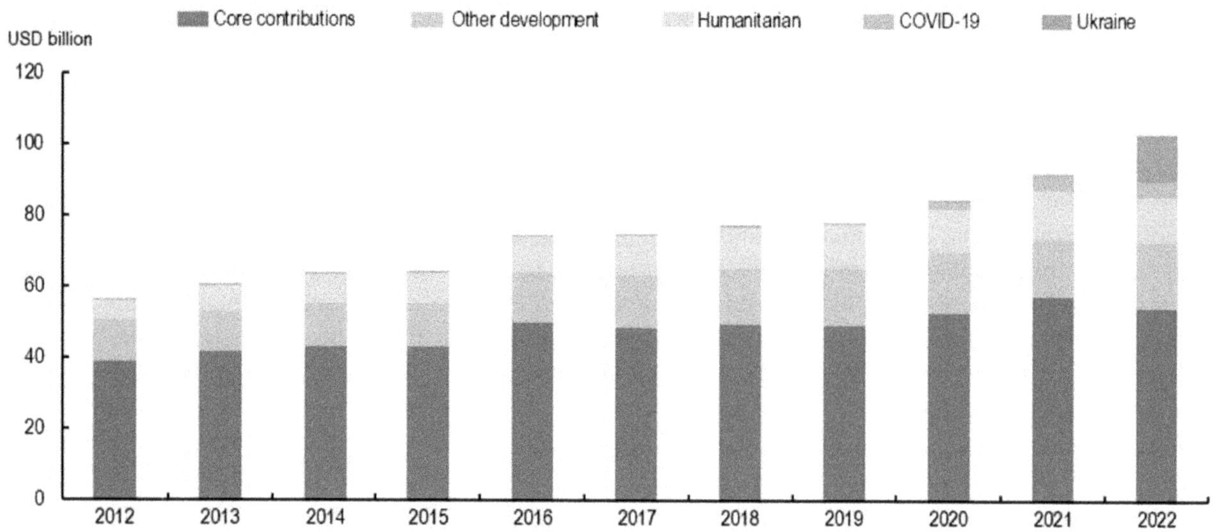


Note: Calculations based on DAC countries' gross disbursements, in 2022 constant prices. Contributions earmarked for humanitarian aid correspond to those reported under CRS sector codes 720, 730 and 740. Contributions earmarked for COVID-19 correspond to those reported under the purpose code 12264. Contributions earmarked for Ukraine are those reported under the recipient code 85.
Source: OECD (2024[11]), OECD Data Explorer, *Members' total use of the multilateral system* (database), http://data-explorer.oecd.org/s/s.

**To deliver the global sustainable development agenda effectively, it is essential that multilateral organisations are resourced in a way that enables them to tackle long-term development challenges.** While the multilateral development system's ability to respond swiftly to emergencies and crises is an important feature, integrating a long-term perspective within such interventions is also increasingly important (Box 3.1). In addition, maintaining a focus on other key sustainable development goals requiring a long-term horizon, such as poverty reduction and climate, is equally important. As discussed in Section 3.2, the recent emphasis on crisis response should not distract from the need to invest in the system, ensuring that multilateral organisations can help developing countries achieve these vital long-term objectives.

### Box 3.1. Tailoring multilateral approaches to an increasingly fragile world

A key strength of the multilateral development system lies in its ability to respond to fragile, crisis and conflict situations. Even without considering the war in Ukraine and the Israel-Hamas conflict, fragility is increasing globally, with projections indicating that by 2030, 86% of the world's extreme poor will be living in fragile contexts (OECD, 2022[8]). Most crises are protracted, highlighting the importance of strategic approaches involving development or peace programming, rather than purely short-term humanitarian aid.

**Many crises demand a long-term perspective to funding and strategies.** Effective crisis responses require organisations operating across the humanitarian, development and peace nexus to look beyond traditional humanitarian sectors and combine their humanitarian funding with longer-term strategies linked to development objectives and broader concerns. Many multilateral organisations have adapted their strategies in recognition of this. The development of an explicit fragility strategy has become the norm among legacy IFIs, including the World Bank Group, the IMF, and the African Development Bank. Many UN agencies have adhered to the DAC Recommendation on the Humanitarian-Development-Peace Nexus (OECD, 2019[9]). The increased number of financing institutions that have started to tailor their work to the needs of fragile contexts, and their expanded role across the humanitarian, development and peace nexus, should be welcomed, supported and reinforced through the ongoing multilateral reform process. Maintaining this focus will be important in the context of the increasing financialisation of the system, which involves increased lending – a modality that can be more difficult to apply in fragile and low-income contexts.

**It is essential to ensure that multilateral organisations are resourced in a way that enables them to frame their interventions within an adaptable and longer-term strategy.** This involves promoting the use of unearmarked funding mechanisms for humanitarian purposes, such as the UN-led Central Emergency Response Fund, and softly earmarked pooled funds, such as the Joint SDG Fund. Although earmarked contributions are vital for the system's capacity to pivot from one crisis to another, a heavy reliance on earmarking, including to multilateral agencies' own crisis response plans, can undermine the very flexibility required in crisis and fragile situations. It can also impact the UN Resident Co-ordinator's role of driving greater coordination and prioritisation of development efforts across humanitarian, development and peace actors.

**Recently, there has also been a notable shift in the type of activities driving donors' earmarking practices.** Historically, humanitarian assistance accounted for a large share of earmarked contributions within the multilateral development system, reflecting the important role of multilateral organisations in delivering humanitarian aid. In recent years, however, earmarked contributions have increasingly been influenced by other crisis response activities. The first major shift occurred with the COVID-19 crisis, in 2020, which required increased funding for vaccine and other health-related activities (Figure 3.5). As a result, contributions earmarked for humanitarian aid declined by 7% between 2019 and 2020 while other earmarked contributions, including COVID-19 control activities, registered a 20% increase. This trend continued in 2021 and most of 2022, driven by support for Ukraine channelled through the main IFIs. For instance, between 2021 and 2022, contributions earmarked for humanitarian purposes rose slightly, by 5%, while other earmarked contributions peaked by 66%, driven by support for Ukraine.

Figure 3.5. Humanitarian aid does not drive the recent peak in earmarked contributions

DAC members' contributions earmarked for humanitarian assistance versus other sectors, 2012-22

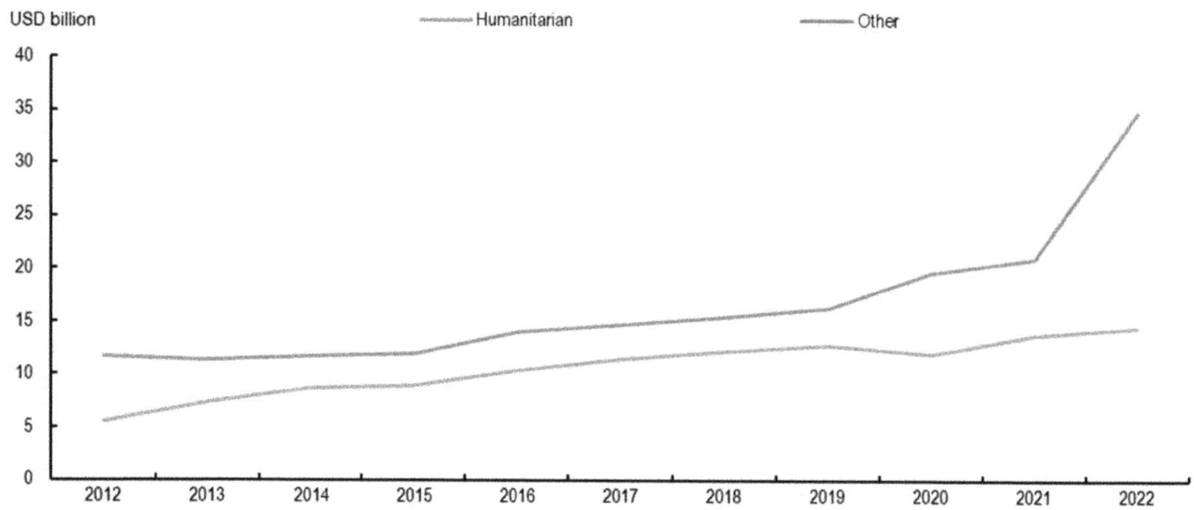


Note: Calculations are based on DAC countries' gross disbursements, in 2022 constant prices. Contributions earmarked for humanitarian aid correspond to those reported under CRS sector codes 720, 730 and 740.
Source: OECD (2024[1]), OECD Data Explorer, *Members' total use of the multilateral system* (database), http://data-explorer.oecd.org/s/s.

### *Donor contributions vary significantly across the multilateral development system, reflecting contrasting resource mobilisation strategies*

**DAC members' contributions to the UNDS and vertical funds have increased in recent years, largely driven by crises.** The traditional funding model of these institutions, relying largely on contributions from their members, led to a substantial increase in funding to meet the additional needs generated by these crises. For instance, funding to the UNDS more than doubled between 2012 and 2022, from USD 19.0 billion to USD 41.9 billion (Figure 1.6). Contributions to vertical funds, which had remained relatively flat until 2019, surged by 125% and 34% in 2020 and 2021, respectively, mainly due to the COVID-19 pandemic. However, in 2022, funding to vertical funds declined by 29%, returning close to 2020 levels.

**By contrast, DAC members' contributions to MDBs have remained relatively flat over the past decade, contributing to their growing reliance on financial innovation.** This is in line with previous analyses showing that donor contributions to the concessional windows of the main MDBs have stagnated or slightly declined in recent replenishments (OECD, 2022[2]). The trend of flat or declining contributions to MDBs stands in stark contrast to their growing outflows over the same period, discussed in greater detail in Chapter 4. This divergence explains the increasing reliance on financial innovation to boost MDBs' financing capacity, a trend further reinforced by ongoing reforms that demand these institutions to do more with the same or even fewer resources, and which emphasises the optimisation of their balance sheets and the use of innovative financial instruments. Ultimately, these trends result in a financialisation of the system, characterised by a growing dependence on financial instruments, financial markets, financial motives and financial institutions for managing and implementing development co-operation activities.

**Figure 3.6. Funding to the UNDS is rising while MDBs need to innovate to compensate for flat donor contributions**

DAC members' contributions by multilateral organisation category, 2012-22

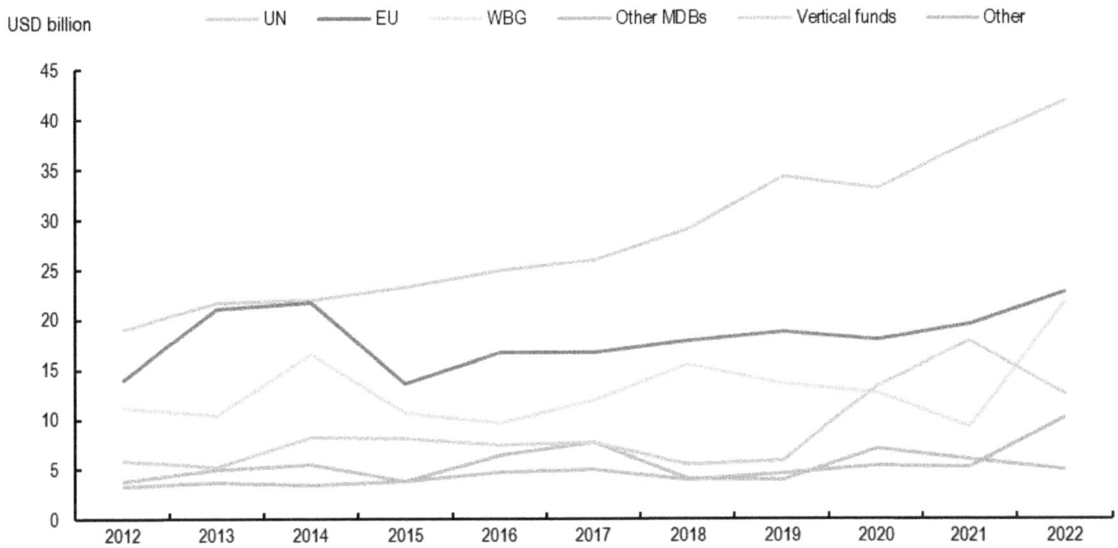


Note: Calculations are based on DAC countries' gross disbursements, in 2022 constant prices. Contributions include both core and earmarked funding.
Source: OECD (2024[1]), OECD Data Explorer, *Members' total use of the multilateral system* (database), http://data-explorer.oecd.org/s/s.

**While the financialisation of the multilateral development system has been beneficial for increasing MDB financing capacity, it also poses certain challenges.** Financial innovation is essential for leveraging additional resources but should not overshadow the critical need for consistent and substantial donor contributions to ensure the sustainability and effectiveness of the multilateral development system. For example, the analysis in Chapter 4 suggests that a prolonged shift towards financial innovation as the primary engine of MDB growth could ultimately affect the concessionality and poverty focus of multilateral development finance.

**To achieve MDB reform targets, donors must complement financial innovation with an increase in high-impact contributions.** The multiplier effect of MDBs' leverage capacity means that increasing contributions to the International Development Association (IDA) and other MDB concessional funds can have a significant impact. For instance, the World Bank Group indicates that IDA can provide four dollars for sustainable development for every dollar contributed by donors (World Bank Group, 2024[10]). Similarly, general capital increases for major MDBs can yield substantial long-term benefits that outweigh the costs for donors. For example, the USD 13 billion paid-in capital increase in 2018 enabled the World Bank Group to boost its lending capacity by about USD 41 billion annually through 2030 (Kenny and Morris, 2021[11]). These examples illustrate the high returns and significant leverage that donor contributions can achieve, highlighting their importance. Conversely, the opportunity cost of not investing through these high-impact and scalable modalities (for example prioritising contributions to trust funds) could be substantial, potentially jeopardising the achievement of ambitious reform targets. Recent and ongoing efforts by MDBs to further increase their leverage should thus be viewed as a compelling reason for donors to increase their contributions, allowing for greater return on their investment, rather than as a substitute.

### *The creation of new funds and windows increases the pace of replenishments and resource competition*

**Over the past decade, the expansion of the multilateral architecture has been primarily driven by the creation of new concessional windows and funds in response to emerging crises.** As shown by a previous edition of this report, which traced the evolution of the multilateral development system since its inception in the 1940s, new multilateral organisations and funding mechanisms have been established over time to address evolving development challenges (OECD, 2020[3]).

**Multi-year replenishments have become the preferred model for many of the newly created multilateral entities and funds.** Among the first to use this funding model were the concessional windows of the main MDBs, namely the World Bank Group's IDA, the African Development Fund (AfDF) and the Asian Development Fund (AsDF), all established between the 1960s and 1970s. A key advantage of the replenishment-based funding model lies in its ability to raise core, unearmarked, voluntary, and multi-year contributions from multiple sources. These characteristics have enabled multilateral entities to secure stable, predictable and flexible funding, while diversifying their donor base to include non-official providers.

**Owing to its success, the replenishment-based funding model has been widely emulated, especially by the numerous vertical funds created since the 1990s.** This new category of issue-specific multilateral entities, often referred to as vertical funds due to their specialised focus, has significantly contributed to the expansion of the multilateral development architecture and the spread of the replenishment-based funding model observed over the past two decades (Figure 3.7). The latest vertical funds, such as the Pandemic Fund and the Loss and Damage Fund currently being operationalised, add to the long list of entities with a replenishment-based funding model.

**Figure 3.7. The creation of new funds adds layers of complexity to the multilateral architecture**

Pledges to MDBs' concessional windows and vertical funds' replenishments, in USD billion

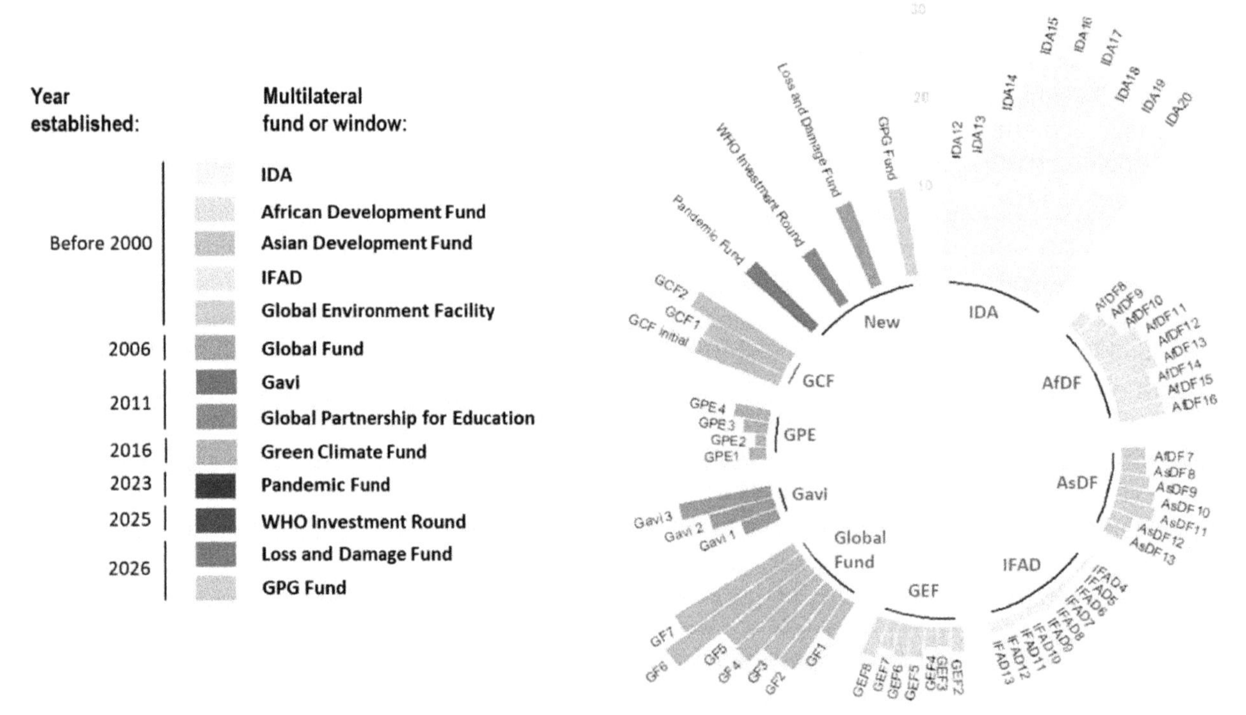


Source: Calculations based on replenishment documents from the following MDBs and vertical funds: International Development Association (IDA), African Development Fund (AfDF), Asian Development Fund (AsDF), International Fund for Agricultural Development (IFAD), Global Environment Facility (GEF), Global Fund, Gavi (the Vaccine Alliance), Global Partnership for Education (GPE) and Green Climate Fund (GCF).

**Some more established entities are also adopting or considering a similar replenishment-based funding model to mitigate their funding vulnerabilities.** The World Health Organization (WHO), for example, whose funding reform process was examined in the previous edition of this report (OECD, 2022[2]), will launch the first WHO Investment Round in 2025. This new replenishment mechanism aims to enhance its funding model, which was partly blamed for the WHO's challenges in addressing the COVID-19 pandemic effectively. Among other goals, the WHO Investment Round is expected to improve the share of core contributions within the organisation's funding mix, which has traditionally relied heavily on non-core earmarked contributions, at the expense of budget predictability and flexibility.

**The newer funds compete for donors' resources with other funding mechanisms with similar replenishment-based funding models**. Over time, the attractiveness of the replenishment-based funding model has resulted in its widespread adoption by new multilateral entities, which end up competing for attention and resources from a limited pool of key multilateral donors (Table 3.1). For example, recent research has highlighted the risk of "replenishment traffic jams" due to the large number of such replenishment exercises now occurring each year (Keller, Landers and Martinez, 2024[12]).

## Table 3.1. Replenishments in the multilateral development system rely on a few major official providers

Top three donors to the main multilateral funds or windows, 2020-22

| | Largest donor | Second largest donor | Third largest donor |
|---|---|---|---|
| **IDA** | United States | Japan | United Kingdom |
| **AfDF** | Japan | United Kingdom | Canada |
| **AsDF** | Japan | Australia | United States |
| **IFAD** | Germany | France | Canada |
| **GEF** | Germany | Japan | United States |
| **GCF** | France | United Kingdom | Germany |
| **Global Fund** | United States | United Kingdom | Germany |
| **Gavi** | United States | Germany | Japan |

Note: Calculations are based on DAC countries' gross disbursements, in 2022 constant prices. International Development Association (IDA), African Development Fund (AfDF), Asian Development Fund (AsDF), International Fund for Agricultural Development (IFAD), Global Environment Facility (GEF), Global Fund, Gavi (the Vaccine Alliance), and Green Climate Fund (GCF).
Source: OECD (2024[1]), OECD Data Explorer, *Members' total use of the multilateral system* (database), http://data-explorer.oecd.org/s/s.

**In the long run, the growing competition for a limited pool of donor resources creates clear winners and losers**. Over the past decade, this dynamic has particularly affected the concessional windows of legacy MDBs, which have experienced a stagnation in donor contributions, in stark contrast to the rising volume of contributions attracted by the main vertical funds (Figure 3.8). One possible, albeit partial, explanation is that donors are increasingly drawn to vertical funds with specialised mandates, greater visibility among the public and simpler impact metrics. However, this trend also suggests that without a corresponding increase in the overall pool of donor resources, legacy institutions may continue to struggle in their replenishment efforts, potentially undermining their ability to address long-term development challenges effectively. This gap could be filled by an increase in financial support from DAC members, explored in Section 3.2., or from an expansion of the role played by emerging donors, examined in Section 3.3.

**Figure 3.8. The concessional windows of the legacy MDBs compete for resources with the vertical funds created over the past two decades**

Evolution of replenishment pledges, latest versus third-to-last replenishment

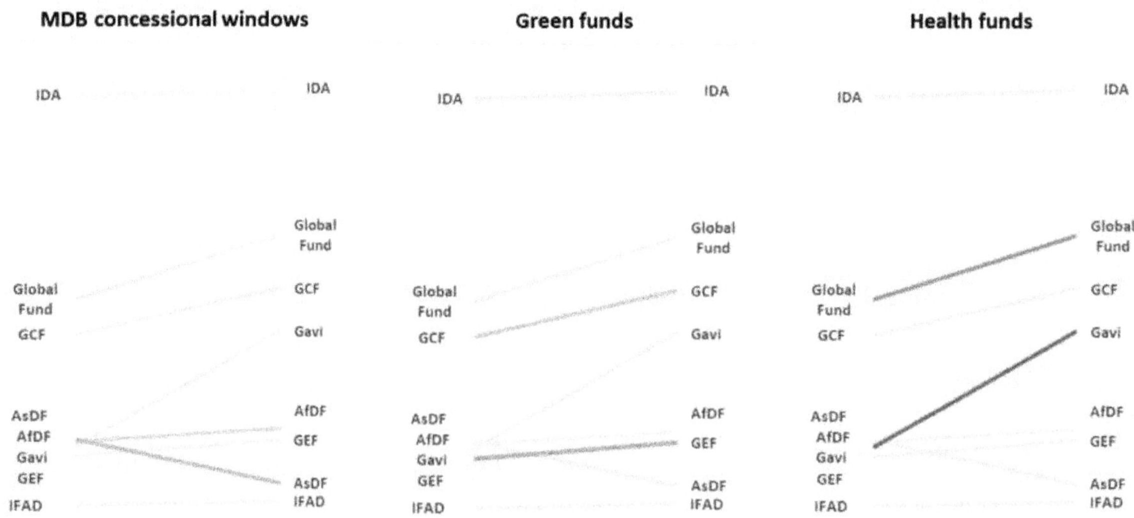


Note: The comparison uses the third-to-last replenishment as baseline (not the penultimate) to avoid using the years of the COVID-19 pandemic as baselines. The lines represent the evolution of replenishment pledges (volume) between the latest and the third-to-last replenishment.
Source: Authors' calculations based on replenishment documents for the following MDBs and vertical funds: International Development Association (IDA), African Development Fund (AfDF), Asian Development Fund (AsDF), Global Environment Facility (GEF), Global Fund, Gavi (the Vaccine Alliance), and Green Climate Fund (GCF).

## DAC members play a vital role through their support to and engagement with the multilateral development system

### *DAC members use various funding strategies to optimise their impact and influence through multilateral contributions*

**A few very large multilateral donors stand out among the DAC membership.** Three DAC providers accounted for half of all DAC contributions to the multilateral development system in 2022 (Figure 3.9). The United States alone represented 26% of total DAC contributions, followed by Germany (17%) and France (7%). In comparison, the 15 smallest DAC providers to the multilateral development system represented only 5% of the total.

**DAC members employ a variety of funding modalities in their multilateral contributions, reflecting their diverse priorities and strategies.** The two largest DAC providers of multilateral contributions, the United States and Germany, exhibit a substantial share of earmarked funding, accounting for 69% and 58% of their total multilateral contributions, respectively. In stark contrast, France, the third largest contributor to the multilateral development system in 2022, predominantly uses core contributions, which constitute 91% of its multilateral funding. This variation in DAC members' approaches is driven by their distinct thematic or geographic priorities, preferences for certain funding modalities, and their desire to exert influence over specific areas of the multilateral agenda. Additionally, the level of their assessed contributions, akin to membership fees based on predefined criteria, also plays a significant role. Historic funding trends further shape these contributions, reflecting DAC members' longstanding commitments.

**Figure 3.9. The United States, Germany and France accounted for half of DAC members' contributions to the multilateral development system in 2022**

DAC members' total use of the multilateral development system (core and earmarked contributions), 2022

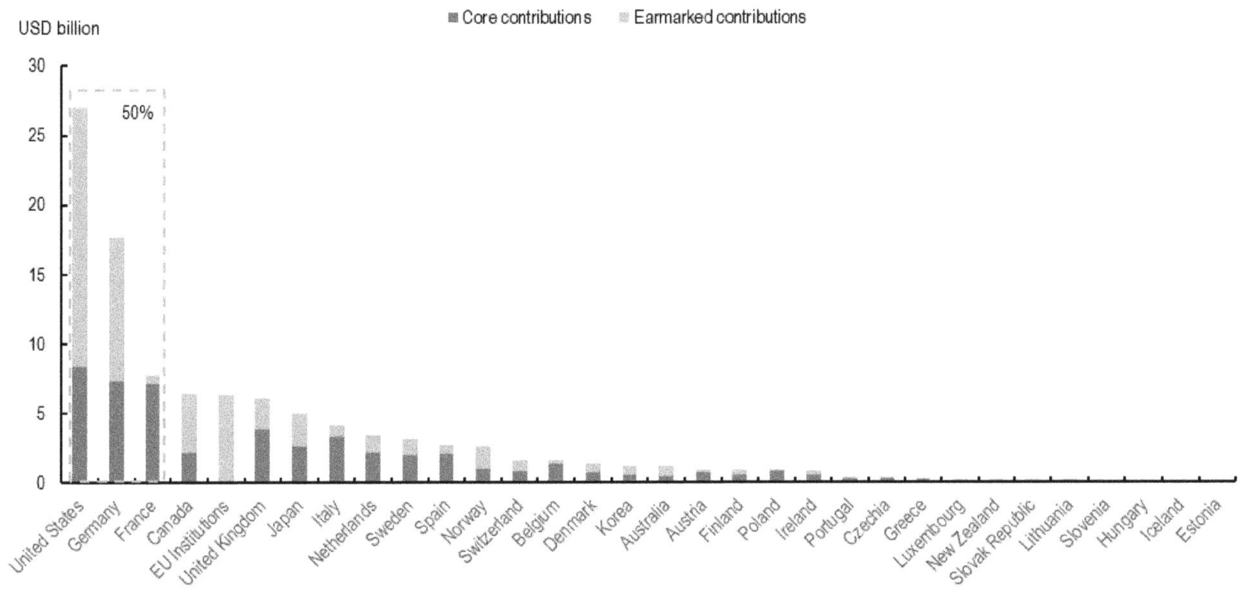


Note: Calculations based on DAC countries' gross disbursements in current prices.
Source: OECD (2024[1]), OECD Data Explorer, *Members' total use of the multilateral system* (database), http://data-explorer.oecd.org/s/s.

**A large majority of DAC members have recently increased their multilateral contributions.** Between 2021 and 2022, only six DAC members reduced their contributions compared to the 2019-2020 period (Figure 3.10). In contrast, the other 26 members all increased their volume of contributions, though the extent of these increases varied. For example, the United States, Germany and Canada recorded the largest volume increases in multilateral contributions, with all three boosting their contributions through earmarked funding. In terms of percentage change, the United States led with a 48% increase, followed by Canada with 42% and Iceland with 40%. This trend of rising multilateral contributions across the DAC membership underscores a broad commitment to supporting developing countries in navigating successive and overlapping crises. This is particularly noteworthy in the global context of budgetary constraints, including in many DAC countries.

**Figure 3.10. More than 80% of DAC members have increased their multilateral contributions since 2019, although levels vary**

Change in DAC members' total use of the multilateral development system (core and earmarked contributions), 2019-20 versus 2021-22

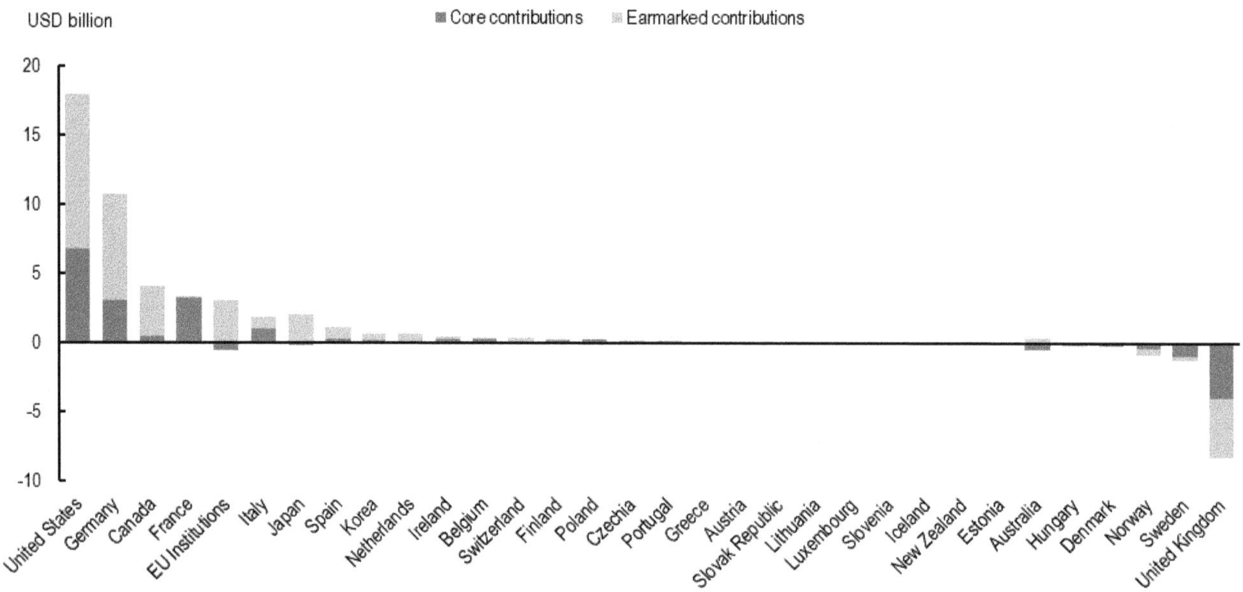


Note: Calculations are based on gross disbursements, in 2022 constant prices.
Source: OECD (2024[1]), OECD Data Explorer, *Members' total use of the multilateral system* (database), http://data-explorer.oecd.org/s/s.

**The volume of DAC countries' of multilateral contributions does not directly correlate with their gross national income (GNI).** Some countries, despite not being among the largest providers to multilateral organisations, contribute more than their fair share relative to their GNI. As highlighted in a previous edition of this report, this is especially the case for Nordic countries, all of which provided more than double their share of the DAC GNI in 2022 (Figure 3.11) (OECD, 2020[3]). Germany, the second largest multilateral contributor, also provides more than twice its corresponding share of ODA. However, this pattern does not hold for all major providers. For instance, the United States, despite being the largest contributor to multilateral organisations among the DAC membership, contributes significantly less than its share of the DAC GNI might suggest.

**Figure 3.11. The largest DAC providers do not necessarily contribute their "fair share" of funding to the multilateral development system**

Contributions to multilateral organisations relative to countries' share in the overall DAC GNI, 2020-22 average

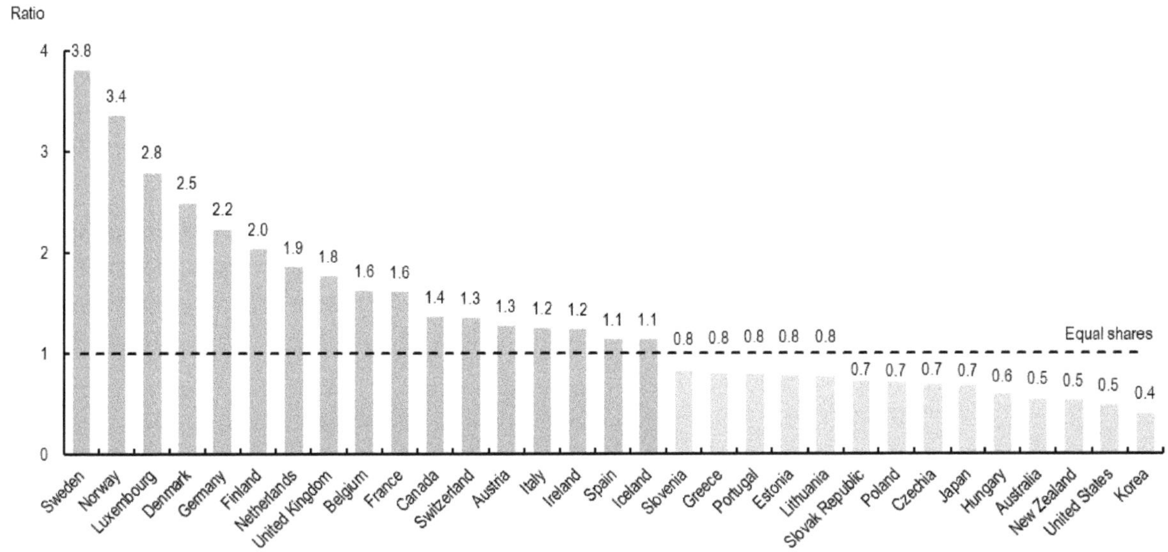


Note: Calculations are based on gross disbursements, in 2022 constant prices, and include both core and earmarked contributions. The values shown for each DAC country represent the volume of their multilateral contributions relative to a scenario where each country contributes to the multilateral development system in proportion to its share of the DAC GNI (indicated by the dotted line). Those above the line contribute more than their fair share.
Source: OECD (2024[1]), Members' total use of the multilateral system (database), http://data-explorer.oecd.org/s/s.

**The analysis in this section sheds some light on DAC members' support for the multilateral system, but also shows that no single measure can provide a comprehensive picture of bilateral partners' use of the system.** A more accurate assessment compares providers across multiple metrics and considers the unique characteristics of each provider. By considering a range of factors – including the balance between core versus earmarked funding, the alignment with global priorities, and the historical commitments of each provider – a more nuanced picture of their support to the multilateral development finance emerges. The online profiles of DAC members' use of the multilateral development system (OECD, 2024[13]), and the dashboard of DAC members' earmarked contributions to multilateral organisations (OECD, 2024[14]), offer additional insights, including a more detailed depiction of the funding modalities used, the multilateral entities supported, and the thematic and geographic focus of each DAC member's contributions.

**Beyond data analysis, further work illustrates the extensive influence bilateral providers can exert on multilateral activities through their funding practices and engagement in governing boards.** This includes efforts to ensure multilateral organisations are given the necessary tools, support and incentives to fulfil their mandates in accordance with development effectiveness principles. For example, recent work has highlighted the critical role bilateral providers can play in enabling multilateral organisations to pivot towards locally-led development (Box 3.2).

## Box 3.2. How multilateral actors can drive locally led development

**Recent work has highlighted the critical role that bilateral providers play in enabling multilateral organisations to pivot towards locally led development** (OECD, 2024[15]). There is no consensus amongst bilateral or multilateral providers on what constitutes "local actors" or "locally led development". However, the growing view is that development is considered to be locally led when all people in a given society – from national governments to communities – are agents in their future and when development co-operation providers allocate funds accordingly (OECD, 2024[15]). Multilateral actors promote locally led development, through a range of mechanisms, systems and partnerships.

**Bilateral providers can strengthen multilateral systems and allow for greater inclusivity and flexible procedures that recognise and promote the agency of local actors.** Table 3.2 gives examples of how DAC members can support multilateral actors in the move to locally led development by adapting their own behaviour, as members of governing boards and in their funding practices.

### Table 3.2. DAC members can help multilateral actors shift to locally led development

| *At capital* | *Board level* | *Partner country level* |
|---|---|---|
| Delegate authority to country offices and equip them to engage with multilateral partners in-country.<br>Support formal roles for local stakeholders as agents primarily responsible for defining priorities, and standards involved in framing, design, delivery and accountability of multilateral programming.<br>Consider staff exchanges with multilateral organisations to build the conditions to support locally led development,<br>Accept higher overhead and administrative costs for multilateral support.<br>Promote dialogue on risk sharing from the start: | Include local voices.<br>Push for simplified reporting and lighter operating procedures.<br>Incentivise multilateral actors to increase staff numbers in partner countries.<br>Set out a clear statement of purpose on locally led development and integrate it into strategic policy documents and monitoring requirements.<br>Review risk appetite statement on what risks a multilateral actor is willing to accept.<br>Talk openly about risk tolerance.<br>Fund the due diligence operations of multilateral entities.<br>Support multilateral organisations to practise local procurement wherever appropriate. | Encourage and allow multilateral partners to plan sufficient time to listen and budget for sufficient resources.<br>Create the right conditions for local authorities and actors to sit on programme steering committees.<br>Agree joint outcomes with multilateral actors based on local results frameworks to co-ordinate approaches and incentivise collaboration.<br>Ensure overhead costs are systematically accessed and used by local actors.<br>Harmonise support to decentralisation efforts.<br>Ensure that multilateral actors support local governance and work with municipalities/ communities. |

Source: OECD (2024[15]), *From global to local: Multilateral actors and the pivot to locally led development*, https://one.oecd.org/document/DCD(2024)23/en/pdf?sessionId=1723453398474 .

### *Long-term investment in the multilateral development system will help it deliver expanded mandates*

**DAC members vary significantly in their use of, and investment in, the multilateral development system.** For example, the share of DAC members' multilateral contributions in their gross ODA, which reflects their use of the multilateral system, ranges from 21% in Japan to 78% in the Slovak Republic (Figure 3.12). Similarly, the share of DAC members' core contributions in their total use of the multilateral system, a measure of their investment in the system, ranges from 37% in Canada to 98% in Poland.

**The overall trend suggests increasing use of, but reduced investment in, the multilateral development system.** As the analysis in Section 1.1 shows, the importance of the multilateral development system as a channel for DAC members' ODA has increased significantly over the past decade. Between 2010 and 2012, DAC members' total use of the multilateral development system accounted for 38% of their gross ODA. By 2020-2022, this figure had risen to 44%, representing a 6% increase. However, this increased use has been accompanied by a decline in the share of core contributions in DAC members' funding to multilateral organisations, which dropped by 11% over the same period, from 69% over 2010-2012 to 58% over 2020-2022. This trend, also seen in the analysis in Section 2.1, suggests that while DAC members are making greater use of the multilateral development system, they are shifting towards more earmarked funding. This shift underscores the need for a balanced approach to funding that ensures the sustainability and effectiveness of the multilateral development system in the long term.

## Figure 3.12. The multilateral system is being used more but invested in less

Core contributions (% of total use of the multilateral system) and total use of the multilateral system (% of gross ODA), 2010-12 and 2020-22 averages

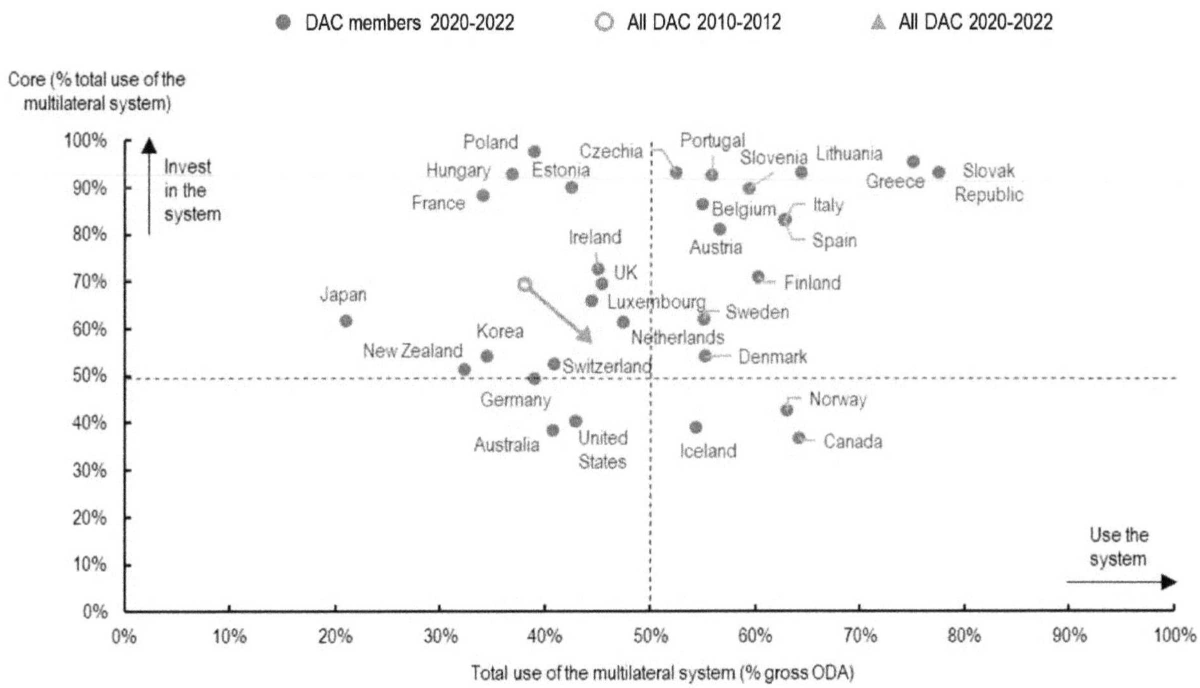


Note: Calculations are based on DAC countries' gross disbursements, in 2022 constant prices.
Source: OECD (2024[1]), OECD Data Explorer, *Members' total use of the multilateral system* (database), http://data-explorer.oecd.org/s/s.

**The erosion of core contributions is visible across the DAC membership.** The ratio between core and earmarked contributions is important because it reflects the balance of flexible, predictable funding versus donor-driven, ad hoc funding within the system. Between 2012 and 2022, this ratio decreased substantially – from 2.3 to 1.1 at the DAC level (Figure 3.13, Panel A.). The analysis also reveals that even DAC members known historically for their strong core support, such as France and Portugal, have seen a decline in their ratio of core to earmarked contributions, although they still maintain some of the highest ratios across the membership (Figure 3.13, Panel B.).

## Figure 3.13. Even historic core supporters reduced their share of core contributions

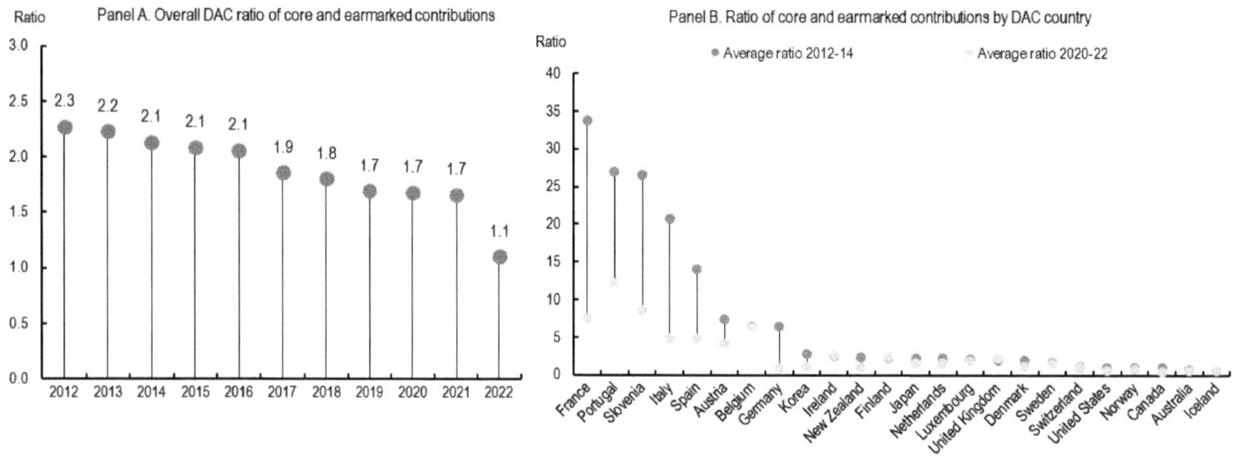


Note: Calculations are based on DAC countries' gross disbursements, in 2022 constant prices.
Source: OECD (2024[1]), OECD Data Explorer, *Members' total use of the multilateral system* (database), http://data-explorer.oecd.org/s/s.

**Looking forward, maintaining a critical mass of core resources will be essential for multilateral organisations to fulfil their mandates effectively.** Core contributions provide the necessary flexibility and stability that these organisations need to respond to evolving global challenges and priorities. Unlike earmarked funds, which are often tied to specific projects or donor preferences, core resources enable multilateral organisations to allocate funding according to strategic priorities set by their governing bodies. This autonomy is crucial for addressing long-term development goals and ensuring that the organisations can maintain essential functions and respond flexibly to emergencies. Moreover, a strong base of core funding helps safeguard the financial health and operational integrity of multilateral institutions, allowing them to undertake strategic planning and monitoring, and maintain a steady course in their mission. As the demand for multilateral support continues to grow, ensuring a robust level of core contributions will be vital for the sustainability and effectiveness of the global development architecture. Recent findings from MOPAN assessments, presented in Box 3.3, support this view.

### Box 3.3. Improving multilateral organisations' funding structures is key to strengthening multilateral effectiveness

**The ability to mobilise and allocate the right level and type of finance is a key driver of multilateral effectiveness.** In a resource-constrained environment, improving the mix of financial resources available to multilateral organisations and developing innovative financing instruments will be increasingly important.

**Although multilateral organisations can adapt to a certain extent to the rise of earmarking, it does create challenges.** Emerging findings from MOPAN assessments and cross-cutting insights show that UN organisations are adapting to greater earmarking by becoming more agile, entrepreneurial and results focused. Yet earmarked funding raises a range of risks and opportunities for multilateral organisations. For example, for organisations working in crises, more efforts are required by funders and multilateral organisations themselves to ensure that forgotten crises are not defunded when new crises hit, and to ensure that resourcing for areas that will save lives and money, such as prevention work, is maintained.

**Organisations also need to reset the relationship with shareholders and funders to move beyond calling for more money and less earmarking towards making a solid case for additional core funds.** They should also tackle – together with member states – issues such as competition for funds and fragmentation, and shift towards a system where finance is an enabler of system-wide collaboration around common goals, including solving pressing global problems like climate change.

**MOPAN's recent assessment of the WHO reveals some good practices** (MOPAN, 2024[16]). It shows how the WHO has made progress towards greater predictability, flexibility and transparency of funding thanks to a regular financing dialogue with key donors, leading to a landmark agreement in May 2023. Under this agreement, member states will increase the level of assessed contributions from 20% to 50% of the WHO's base budget between 2024-25 and 2027-28 (or latest 2029-30). Member states will also increase the length of replenishment rounds, allowing for longer-term investment beyond the current two-year rhythm. The WHO's high level of accountability and transparency in its use of resources, and reporting improvements, have facilitated this process.

Source: MOPAN (2024[16]), *Performance at a Glance: World Health Organization* (WHO).

## Emerging donors are slowly reshaping multilateral institutions' funding base

**Although DAC members continue to play a pivotal role in the multilateral development system, emerging donors are progressively assuming greater prominence.** Previous editions of this report have described that many multilateral organisations have begun to diversify their funding base over the past decade to mobilise more resources from middle-income countries and private foundations, and through innovative financing (OECD, 2020[3]) (OECD, 2022[2]). In the current context of stagnating donor resources and substantial financing needs to achieve the ambitions of the 2030 Agenda, broadening the funding base and accessing additional sources of financing remains a priority for most multilateral institutions.

**Emerging donors bring diverse perspectives, innovative approaches, and alternative priorities to the table, influencing the allocation of resources and the strategic direction of multilateral initiatives.** As their influence grows, the multilateral system faces both opportunities and challenges in accommodating this evolving landscape. This section uses statistical sources drawn from individual multilateral organisations to assess the role of fast-growing non-DAC official providers (hereafter referred to as emerging donors) in the funding of two organisations: 1) the United Nations Development System; and 2) the World Bank Group's concessional window, IDA. While the focus on these institutions does not cover all developments in the multilateral development system, it does offer insights into a significant portion of the system, accounting for nearly half (48%) of total multilateral development finance extended to ODA-eligible countries in 2022.

### *A few emerging donors are becoming important players in the multilateral development system*

**Since the early 2000s, aid from emerging donors has gained significant attention.** The term "emerging donors" does not necessarily refer to newly established aid contributors; rather, it encompasses countries like the People's Republic of China and Saudi Arabia which, despite their long-standing involvement in aid, have garnered attention due to their expanding presence and influence in international relations and development (Kondoh Hisahiro, 2024[17]). Emerging donors in the multilateral system include major economies that have become significant international actors over the past decade such as the BRICS – Brazil, Russia, India, China and South Africa – as well as Argentina, Chile, Indonesia, Israel, Mexico, Saudi Arabia, Türkiye, and the United Arab Emirates (Hughes and Mitchell, 2023[18]).

**While DAC members remain the main funders of the multilateral development system, a few emerging donors have increased their contributions notably.** In line with the trend observed in previous editions of this report, DAC countries accounted for 95% of donor contributions to the UNDS in 2022, while emerging donors contributed approximately 4% and other official donors made up the remaining 1%. Yet, collectively, emerging donors rank as the eighth largest government donor to the UNDS (Figure 3.14). More importantly, at the level of individual donors, some emerging actors – such as China – are gradually carving out a leadership role in the multilateral development system, highlighting their growing influence and commitment to international development.

#### Figure 3.14. As a group, emerging donors are the 8th largest UNDS' government contributor

Top contributions from government donors to the UNDS, 2022

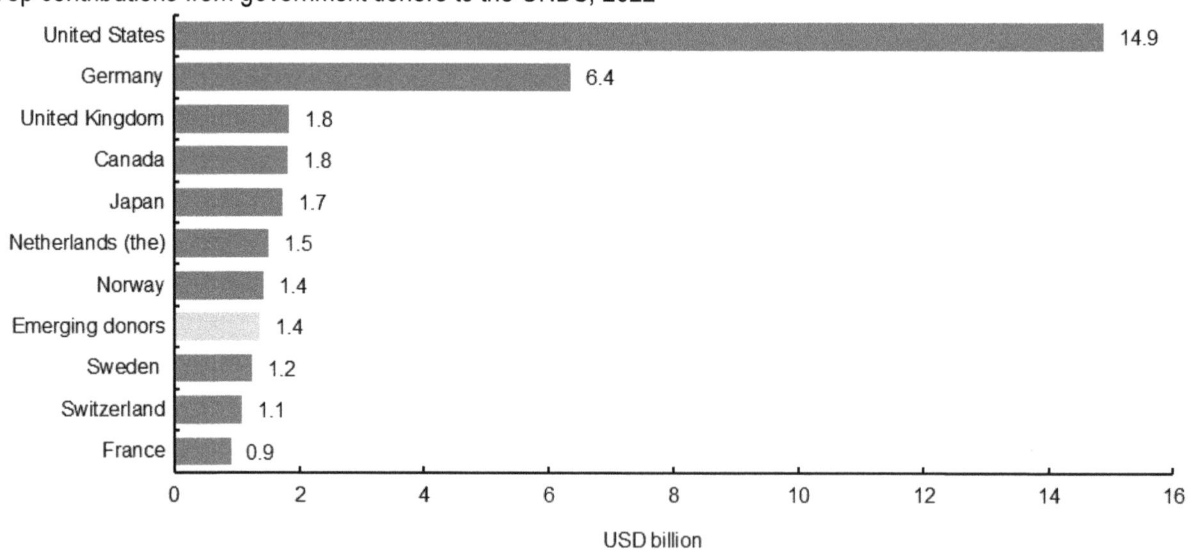


Note: Emerging donors included here are Argentina, Brazil, Chile, China, India, Indonesia, Israel, Mexico, Russia, Saudi Arabia, South Africa, Turkey and the United Arab Emirates (Hughes and Mitchell, 2023[18]). Calculations include core assessed, core voluntary and non-core (earmarked) contributions provided by government donors but exclude non-core local resources.
Source: Authors' calculations based on UNSCEB (2024[19]), *Financial Statistics*, https://unsceb.org/financial-statistics.

**Over the past decade, China has made remarkable progress up the rankings of major donor contributors to the UNDS.** In 2022, the country moved up 8 places to become the 15th largest donor, a significant leap from 23rd in 2012. Other emerging donors, such as Brazil, India, Mexico, Russia, Saudi Arabia, Turkey and the United Arab Emirates, have also secured spots among the UNDS's top 30 contributors. Between 2012 and 2022, some of these countries dramatically increased their contributions: China by 576%, the United Arab Emirates by 367%, India by 196%, and Turkey by 109% (Figure 1.7).

### Figure 3.15. China, the UAE, and India are amongst the largest and fastest-growing donors to the UNDS

Funding to UNDS, 2022, and % change in contributions, 2012 versus 2022

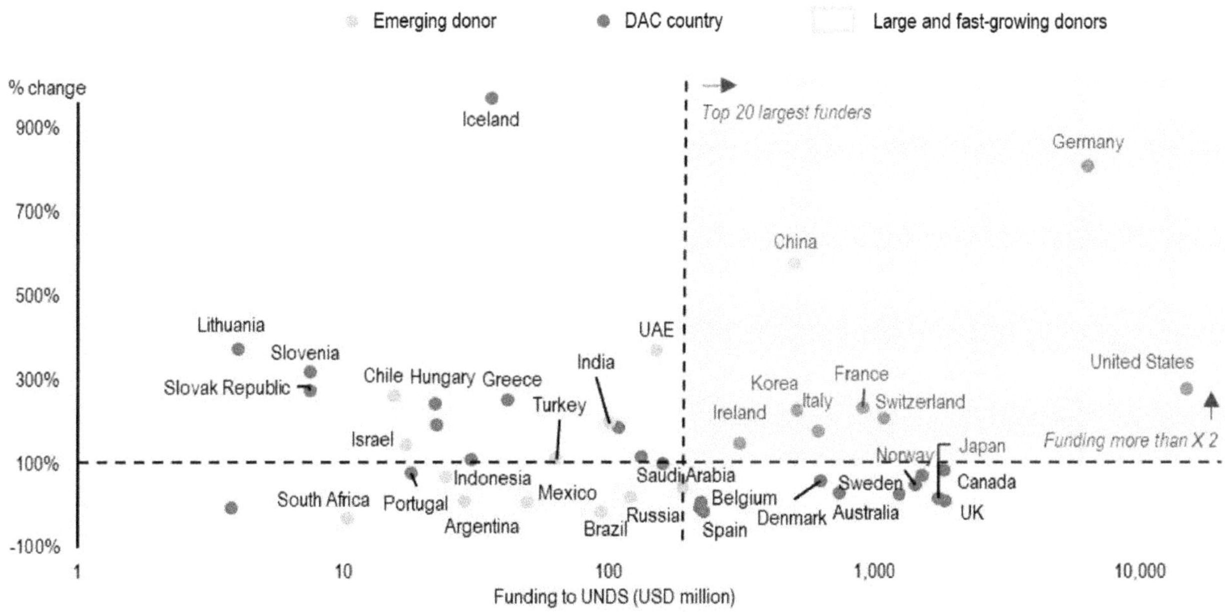


Note: Emerging donors included here are Argentina, Brazil, Chile, China, India, Indonesia, Israel, Mexico, Russia, Saudi Arabia, South Africa, Turkey and the United Arab Emirates (Hughes and Mitchell, 2023[18]). Calculations include core assessed, core voluntary and non-core (earmarked) contributions provided by government donors but exclude non-core local resources.
Source: Authors' calculations based on UNSCEB (2024[19]), *Financial Statistics*, https://unsceb.org/financial-statistics.

**The trend is similar for the World Bank Group, with some emerging donors significantly increasing their contributions to IDA replenishments.** Notably, China and Saudi Arabia have boosted their contributions by 763% and 566% respectively between IDA16 and IDA20 (completed in 2010 and 2022 respectively). Furthermore, China, Saudi Arabia and India were among the top 20 largest contributors to IDA20 (Figure 3.16). India's rise is particularly remarkable, having rapidly become one of the largest IDA contributors despite not even being a contributor to IDA's 16th replenishment in 2010.

**Figure 3.16. China and Saudi Arabia are amongst the largest and fastest-growing donors to IDA replenishments**

Contributions to IDA20, 2022, and % change in contributions, IDA16 in 2010 vs IDA20 in 2022

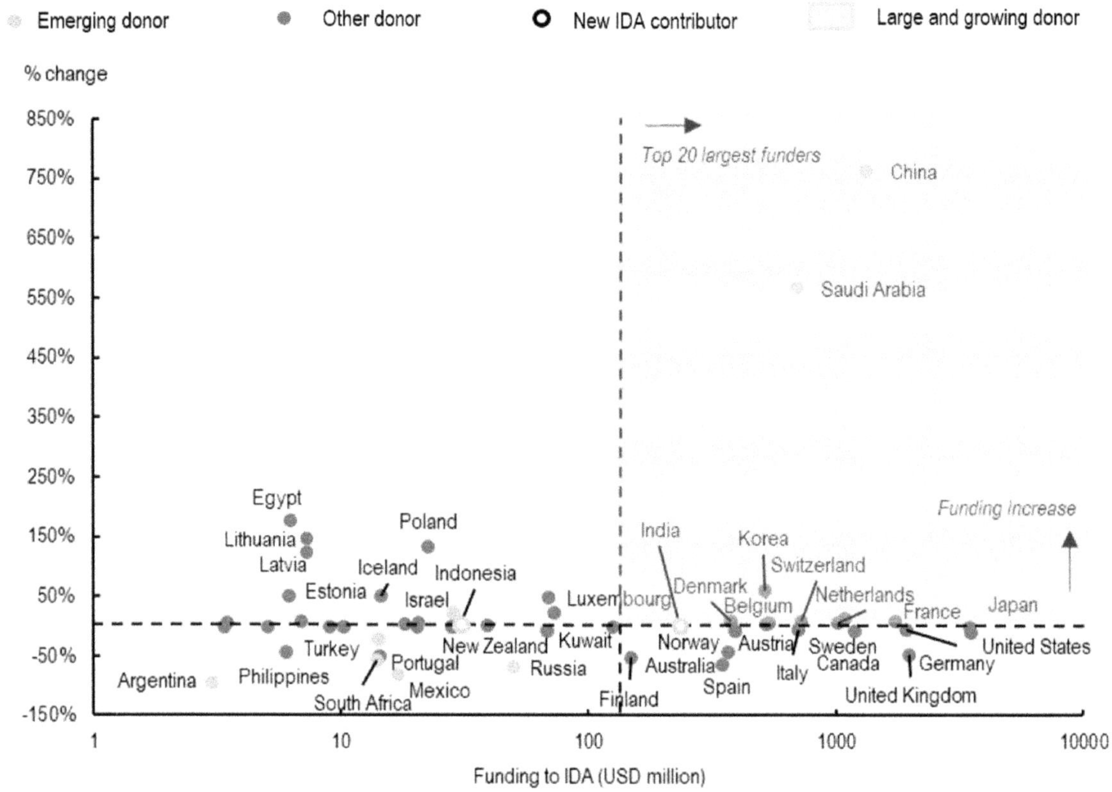


Note: Emerging donors included here are Argentina, Brazil, Chile, China, India, Indonesia, Israel, Mexico, Russia, Saudi Arabia, South Africa, Turkey and the United Arab Emirates (Hughes and Mitchell, 2023[18]). Calculations include all DAC countries, and exclude other non-government donors, such as NGOs, private sector, and other multilateral organisations. New IDA contributors refers to donors that were not yet contributing to IDA in 2010 (IDA16) and for which the percentage change in contributions cannot be calculated.
Source: Authors' calculations based on World Bank Group (2024[20]), *IDA20 Replenishment*, https://ida.worldbank.org/en/replenishments/ida20-replenishment.

**The decision by emerging donors to invest in the IDA reflects a rational strategy to maximise their influence within the multilateral development system.** It is noteworthy that some emerging donors choose to start contributing to the IDA and then rapidly scale up their contributions in subsequent replenishments, rather than increasing their voluntary contributions to the UNDS, an institution where emerging donors are historically seen as having a stronger voice. This can be explained by the fact that investing in the IDA grants these donors a seat at the negotiation table, enabling them to influence the IDA's strategic direction and content, including its geographical and thematic priorities. Moreover, given the international attention placed on IDA replenishments, this engagement is an effective way for emerging donors to gain visibility and clout. Contributions to the IDA not only enhance emerging donors' decision-making power within one development finance institutions, but also increase their overall standing and influence within the global development landscape.

**While in aggregate terms DAC members remain by far the largest donor contributors to the UNDS and IDA, their influence is declining as a share of all sources of funding.** For example, the previous edition of this report revealed that donor contributions represented a decreasing share of the total envelope of the MDBs' concessional windows (OECD, 2022[2]) due to the MDBs' capacity to mobilise financing from other sources (market borrowing in IDA's hybrid model is one example). The 2022 edition of the report also highlighted the growing role of private contributions in the UNDS, although their importance varies significantly across UNDS entities.

### *Emerging donors' funding patterns reflect different strategies to leverage multilateral finance to advance their global or regional agendas*

**The mix of emerging donors' funding modalities differs significantly from that of DAC members.** Core contributions represent about two-thirds of emerging donors' total contributions to the UNDS, compared to only 17% for DAC member countries (Figure 3.17). The difference becomes even more pronounced when examining core assessed contributions: these constitute a mere 5% of DAC members' funding to the UNDS, but a substantial 55% for emerging donors.

#### Figure 3.17. Emerging donors and DAC members have different funding patterns

UNDS funding mix by provider type, 2022

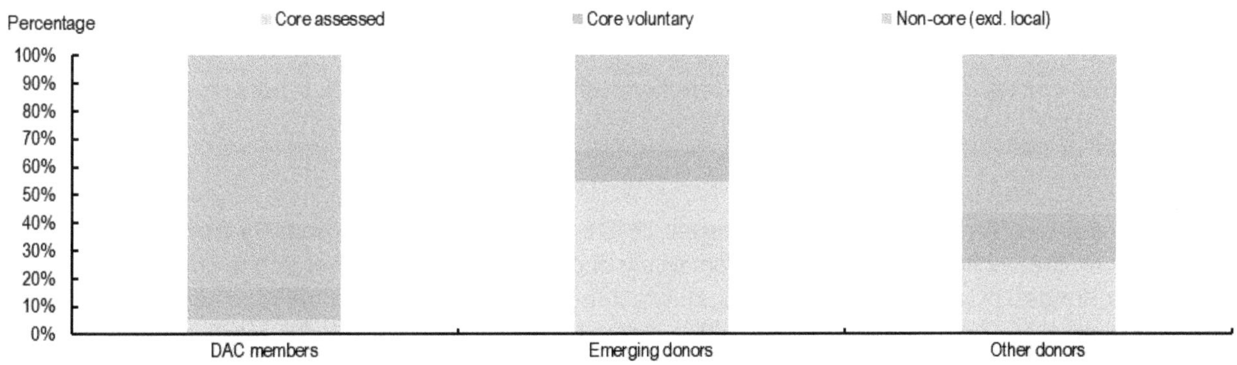


Note: Emerging donors included here are Argentina, Brazil, Chile, China, India, Indonesia, Israel, Mexico, Russia, Saudi Arabia, South Africa, Turkey and the United Arab Emirates (Hughes and Mitchell, 2023[18]). Calculations include all DAC countries, and exclude other non-government donors, such as NGOs, private sector, and other multilateral organisations.
Source: Authors' calculations based on UNSCEB (2024[19]), *Financial Statistics*, https://unsceb.org/financial-statistics.

**An analysis of individual emerging donors shows that their varying funding patterns reflect their priorities and agendas.** The United Arab Emirates and Saudi Arabia stand out among emerging donors for their larger share of earmarked contributions in their overall contributions – 85% and 66% respectively (Figure 3.18). This largely reflects a deliberate strategy to direct funds towards specific regional needs within the Middle East, allowing these countries to address targeted priorities and exert influence within their immediate geopolitical sphere. In contrast, other emerging donors such as China and Brazil display a markedly different pattern, with 85% and 86% of their funding to the UNDS respectively consisting of core contributions, reflecting in part their desire to shape the broader, global development agenda.

## Figure 3.18. Among emerging donors, only Saudi Arabia and the UAE make greater use of earmarked than core contributions to the UNDS

Emerging donors' contributions to the UNDS, 2022

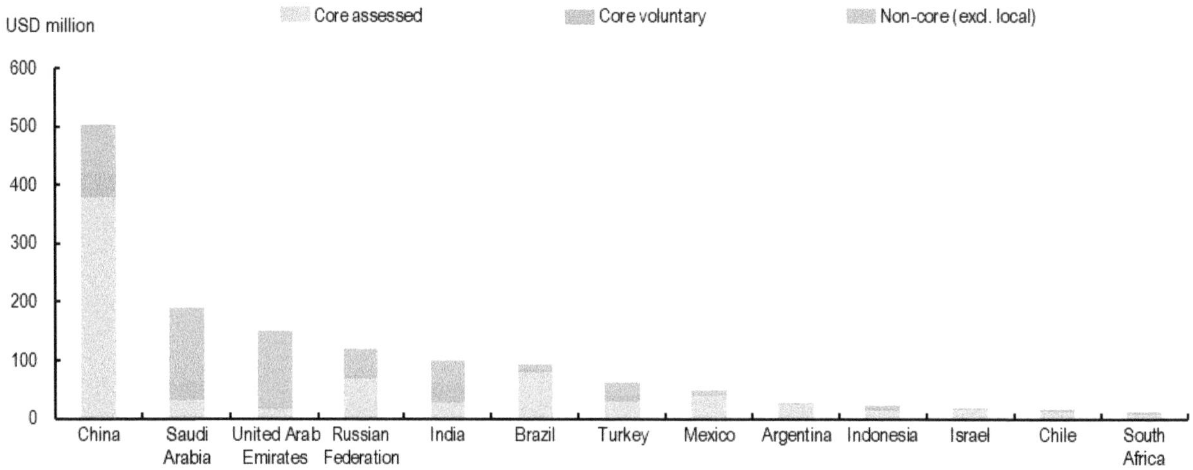


Note: Calculations include all DAC countries, and exclude other non-government donors, such as NGOs, private sector, and other multilateral organisations.
Source: Authors' calculations based on UNSCEB (2024[19]), *Financial Statistics*, https://unsceb.org/financial-statistics.

**Emerging donors' funding allocations across UNDS entities differ significantly from those of DAC members.** In 2022, the largest single recipient entity of contributions from emerging countries was the UN Secretariat (funded by assessed contributions), which accounted for 25% of their total contributions to the UNDS (Figure 3.19, Panel A). In contrast, DAC members' funding to the UN Secretariat only accounted for 2% of their total contributions to the UNDS (Figure 3.19, Panel B). This difference largely stems from the fact that emerging donors tend to provide less voluntary and earmarked funding than DAC members. There are also differences in magnitude: although DAC members' contributions to the UN Secretariat represented only 2% of their total multilateral contributions, this amounted to USD 1,248.8 million. In comparison, emerging donors contributed USD 339.7 million to the UN Secretariat, which, despite representing a quarter of their total multilateral contributions, is significantly lower in absolute terms. This highlights the substantial difference in scale between the contributions of DAC members and emerging donors, even though the latter's strategic preferences shape distinct funding patterns within the UNDS.

**Figure 3.19. Emerging donors and DAC members differ in their contributions to UN entities and shares to the UN Secretariat**

Panel A. Emerging donors' top 10 UNDS contributions (2022)

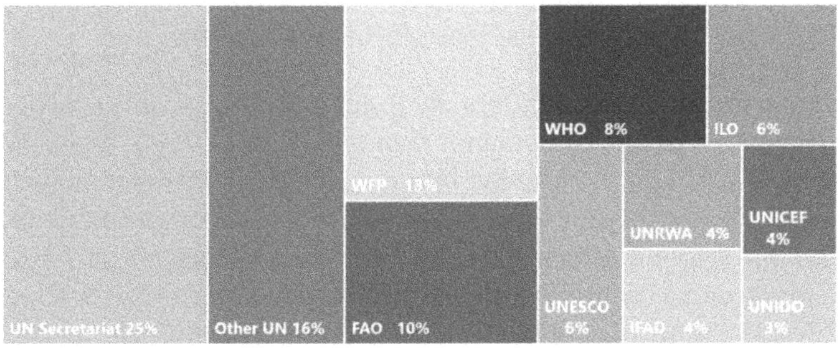


Panel B. DAC members' top 10 UN contributions (2022)

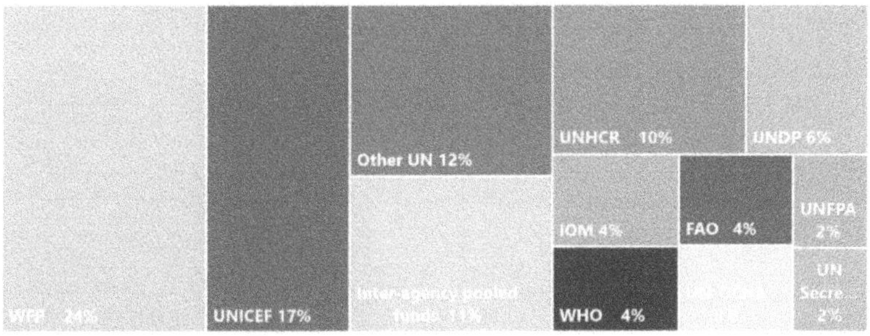


Note: Emerging donors included here are Argentina, Brazil, Chile, China, India, Indonesia, Israel, Mexico, Russia, Saudi Arabia, South Africa, Turkey and the United Arab Emirates (Hughes and Mitchell, 2023[18]). Calculations include all DAC countries, and exclude other non-government donors, such as NGOs, private sector, and other multilateral organisations.
Source: Authors' calculations based on UNSCEB (2024[19]), *Financial Statistics*, https://unsceb.org/financial-statistics.

**Emerging donors are increasingly leveraging the "power of the purse" to secure influence in the UNDS.** Funding serves as a crucial mechanism for countries to assert their influence, and the highest contributions from emerging donors to specific UN entities reveal their strategic priorities. For instance, China's largest contributions go to the UN Secretariat and the FAO, while its earmarked funding prioritises the UN Department for Economic and Social Affairs (UN DESA). This is consistent with China's priorities of securing high-level UN senior management positions: China currently leads both UN DESA and the FAO. Similarly, Saudi Arabia focuses its contributions on the WFP and UNRWA and the United Arab Emirates on the WFP and FAO, reflecting their emphasis on humanitarian assistance in the Middle East region.

**In addition to the volume of their contributions, the funding practices of these emerging donors are becoming a strategic tool to enhance their influence.** These funding allocations not only reflect the priorities of emerging donors but also their capacity to shape the agenda and operations of the UNDS, thereby bolstering their global standing and influence. For instance, by directing significant resources to specific UN entities, emerging donors can prioritise issues aligned with their national interests and policy goals, ensuring these are addressed within the traditional multilateral framework. Funding practices are also increasingly wielded as an instrument of soft power and diplomatic leverage. This was notably exemplified in 2020 when China publicly criticised the United States for its funding arrears with the UN, highlighting the geopolitical dimensions that multilateral funding practices can assume (Fung and Lam, 2022[21]).

**Emerging donors' growing engagement in multilateral development finance provides an opportunity for strengthened outreach and knowledge exchange with the OECD DAC.** Stronger outreach and knowledge exchange could enable emerging donors and OECD DAC members to share their experiences with multilateral development co-operation, and discuss policies as well as the good practices and challenges of being effective partners with multilateral organisations, with a view to collectively ensuring that multilateral organisations are well-equipped to address future challenges.

### *Newer, Southern-led multilateral organisations offer emerging donors an alternative way to influence the direction of multilateral development finance*

**Emerging actors remain minor shareholders in legacy MDBs despite large differences across institutions**. Contributions from emerging countries represent about 33% of total contributions to the Inter-American Development Bank (IADB), 24% to the International Bank for Reconstruction and Development (IBRD), 15% to the Asian Development Bank (ADB), 6% to the European Bank for Reconstruction and Development (EBRD) and 3% to the African Development Bank (AfDB) (Figure 3.20). This contrasts with DAC members, which are collectively majority shareholders in four out of the five main MDBs, namely the EBRD (89%), IBRD (59%), ADB (50%) and IADB (50%).

**Figure 3.20. Emerging donors' shareholdings vary significantly across the legacy MDBs**

Emerging donors' shares of capital in the main MDBs, 2022

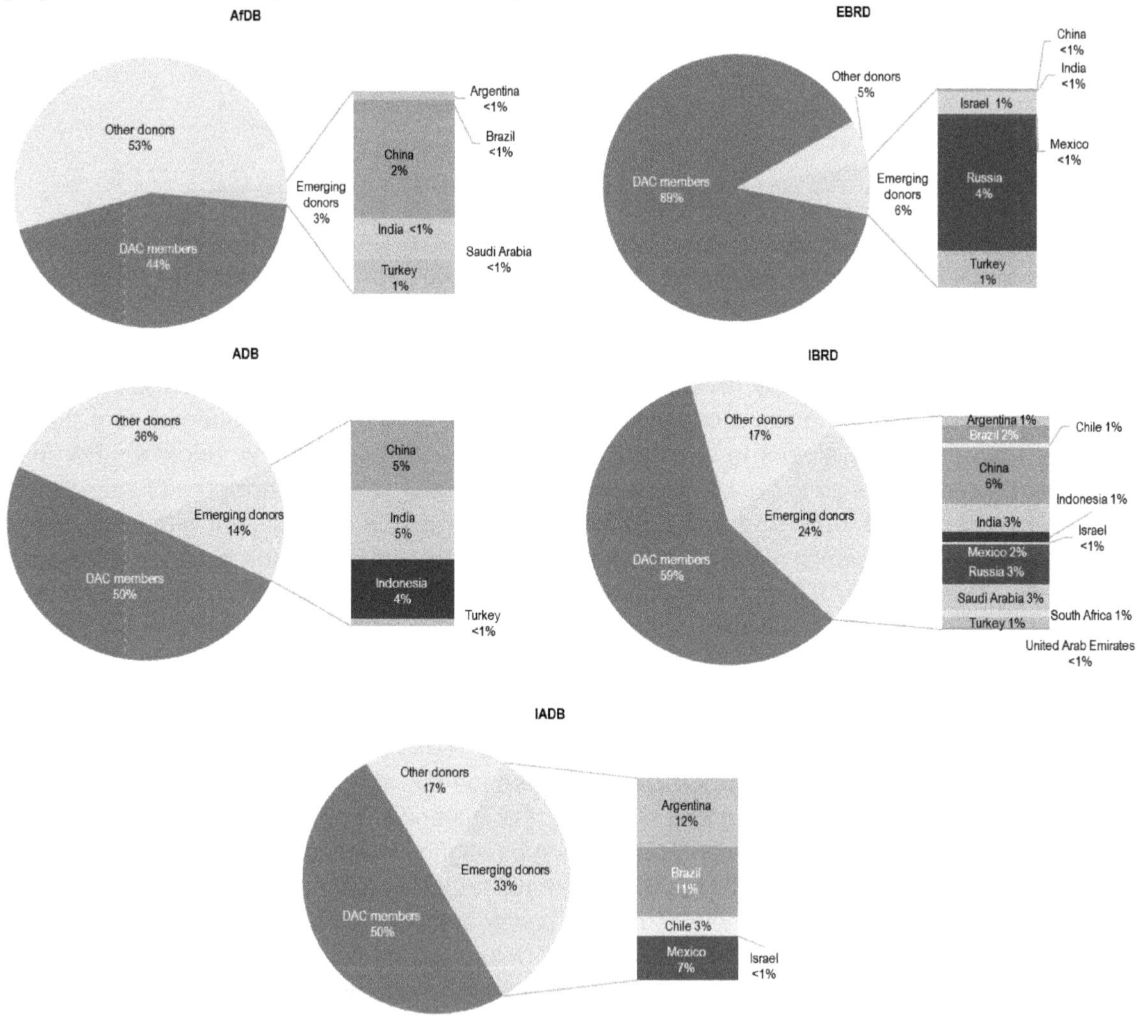


Note: AfDB: African Development Bank; ADB: Asian Development Bank; EBRD: European Bank for Reconstruction and Development; IADB: Inter-American Development Bank; IBRD: International Bank for Reconstruction and Development.
Source: Authors' calculations based on these organisations' official documents.

**Over the past decade, emerging donorship has also materialised through the creation of two new MDBs: the New Development Bank (NDB) and the Asian Infrastructure Investment Bank (AIIB).** Following a proposal by India, the BRICS countries – Brazil, Russia, India, China, and South Africa – established the NDB in 2014. That same year, China and 20 other Asian nations signed an agreement to create the AIIB. The goals of both the NDB and the AIIB are to mobilise resources to address the substantial infrastructure investment gap and promote sustainable development in developing countries (OECD, 2020[3]).

**The establishment of these two new MDBs was widely considered as a significant challenge to what is perceived as a Western-dominated system.** Developing countries had long sought greater representation in multilateral institutions, but progress on voice reform had been considered slow and limited, and legacy institutions were often seen as too bureaucratic and inefficient (Kellerman, 2018[22]). The new MDBs were created with the stated aim to enhance representation for developing countries in the multilateral development system, prioritise infrastructure development, eliminate political considerations from lending decisions, and increase efficiency (Wang, 2019[23]). Unlike in the legacy MDBs, emerging donors hold a majority of the AIIB's and NDB's capital (Figure 3.21).

## Figure 3.21. Emerging donors are the largest shareholders in the newer, Southern-led MDBs

Emerging donors' shares in new development banks, 2021

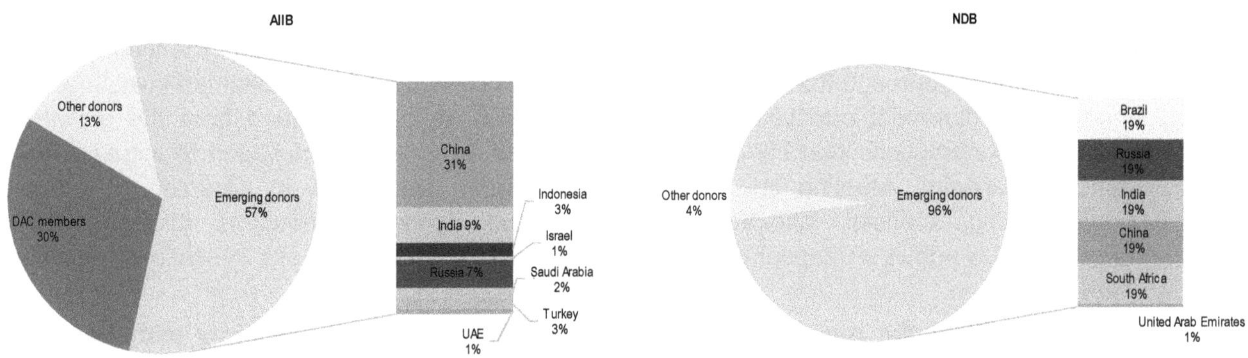


Note: AIIB: Asian Infrastructure Investment Bank; NDB: New Development Bank.
Source: Authors' calculations based on these organisations' official documents.

**The scope of recent calls for MDB reform can partly apply to Southern-led MDBs.** Currently, the discourse on MDB reform has predominantly centred on legacy institutions, especially the World Bank Group. While newer institutions, given their relatively recent establishment, are yet to reach full operational maturity – with the AIIB for example projecting maturity around 2030 – achieving the ambitious goals of the MDB reform agenda will require concerted efforts by all components of the system, including Southern-led MDBs. Excluding them from the reform process risks undermining their potential contribution to this new agenda. Research is highlighting certain areas where Southern MDBs could improve their effectiveness, such as increasing their country presence to engage more robustly with the overall external development finance ecosystem, including private sector actors (Bhattacharya et al., forthcoming[24]).

**Southern-led MDBs are already adapting their operational models to align them better with the evolving needs and demands of their client countries.** Recent evolutions in these newer MDBs point to a notable convergence with the legacy MDB system in some respects. For instance, while the AIIB does not provide concessional finance, it has formally established in 2022 a Special Funds Window for Less Developed Members (SFW), which provides an interest rate buy down – a discount on the regular interest – of its USD-denominated loans. The AIIB has also started to decentralise its operations by setting up an operational hub in Abu Dhabi, moving away from a headquarters-only model. In response to the economic and social challenges posed by the COVID-19 pandemic, Southern-led MDBs are also expanding their financial toolkit to include budget support and social investments, which were previously outside their infrastructure-centric focus. Interestingly, while newer MDBs are starting to embrace concessional finance, legacy MDBs, despite having well-established concessional frameworks, have increasingly focused their interventions on non-concessional finance in recent years. This divergence raises critical questions about the role of legacy MDBs, in which DAC members hold majority stakes, and whether they might be neglecting certain areas, thus leaving newer MDBs to fill these gaps. Ultimately, such dynamics have significant implications for their comparative advantages and the division of labour within the global development finance landscape.

## Key chapter findings and solutions

### *Key findings*

**The chapter has highlighted significant trends and shifts in funding to the multilateral development system (multilateral inflows):**

- **The continued growth in OECD DAC members' use of the multilateral system, reaching record levels in 2022, underscores the system's increasing relevance.** However, this growth is predominantly driven by crisis response funding, with contributions to other long-term development goals remaining relatively stagnant. Despite recent reforms to expand multilateral mandates, these broader objectives are not yet fully reflected in current funding trends. This points to the need for a more integrated approach that balances immediate crisis response with sustained investments in long-term development priorities. Additionally, MDBs have not benefitted from the growth in multilateral contributions and have had to rely instead on financial innovation to increase their financing capacity. Meeting the MDB reform targets presented in Chapter 1 requires complementing financial innovation with increased donor contributions through MDBs' concessional windows or capital increases, which can capitalise on these institutions' multiplier effect.
- **The growing use of the multilateral development system contrasts sharply with declining investment in its core functions.** While DAC members are increasingly channelling funds through multilateral organisations, much of this funding is earmarked for specific crises or projects. Although earmarked contributions can address specific needs, they cannot substitute for core contributions, which are essential for the flexibility and stability of multilateral organisations. Ultimately, a continued shift towards earmarked funding could undermine their capacity to pursue their core mandates effectively. Maintaining a critical mass of core contributions thus remains essential for ensuring the system's ability to respond sustainably to global development challenges.
- **Emerging donors are playing an increasingly influential role, using their financial contributions strategically to shape the agenda and operations of multilateral institutions.** Countries like China and Saudi Arabia have significantly increased their contributions, particularly to organisations like the UNDS and the World Bank Group's IDA, enhancing their global influence. This diversification of funding sources brings new resources and opportunities, potentially enriching the multilateral development system with fresh perspectives and additional financial support, and easing pressures generated by the competition for scarce resources. The growing engagement of emerging donors in multilateral development finance could provide the basis for closer partnerships with the OECD DAC to discuss how to collectively ensure that multilateral organisations are well-equipped to address future challenges.

### *Key recommendations*

**Maximise contributions to high-impact funding mechanisms:** Capitalise on the multiplier effect of multilateral funding mechanisms to achieve initial reform targets by ensuring successful replenishments of MDB concessional windows and global funds. Explore the possibility of additional capital contributions (e.g. to general capital increases or hybrid capital instruments). Ensure that a substantial portion of multilateral development finance remains highly concessional and affordable for the poorest and most vulnerable countries.

**Ensure adequate funding for core strategic functions:** Invest in the core functions of multilateral organisations to maintain their ability to perform their mandates. Adjust the formula and level of UN assessed contributions to reflect member countries' actual economic weight. This can ensure increased, fair share contributions, and help rebalance core and earmarked contributions to the UNDS. Recognising the specificities of each multilateral organisation, bring discussions on funding quality to their governing bodies to complement general UN Funding Compact commitments (following the model of the WHO reform or structured financing dialogues).

**Prioritise flexible funding:** In accordance with UN Funding Compact commitments, prioritise multi-year and flexible funding modalities, such as contributions to multi-donor and inter-agency pooled funds, as these foster co-ordination, reduce fragmentation and enable organisations to adapt to countries' needs.

**Engage with emerging donors on multilateral development finance:** Acknowledge the growing role of some non-DAC donors in the multilateral system. Use existing OECD DAC outreach mechanisms, such as the policy dialogues with Arab and Latin American and Caribbean countries, to discuss insights from OECD analyses on multilateral development finance and effective multilateral development co-operation and to develop common ground for good practices in these areas.

## References


Bhattacharya, D. et al. (forthcoming), *Reforming Southern MDBs: Evidence from country-level practices.* [24]

Hughes, S. and I. Mitchell (2023), *Emerging Actors in the Multilateral System*, Center for Global Development, https://www.cgdev.org/publication/emerging-actors-multilateral-system (accessed on 23 May 2024). [18]

IDOS (ed.) (2024), *Financing the UN system: Status quo, challenges and reform options*, https://ny.fes.de/fileadmin/user_upload/Financing_the_UN_online.pdf. [6]

Institute, L. (ed.) (2022), *Mixed report card: China's influence at the United Nations*, https://www.lowyinstitute.org/publications/mixed-report-card-china-s-influence-united-nations. [21]

Keller, J., C. Landers and N. Martinez (2024), *The 2024-2025 Replenishment Traffic Jam: Are We Headed for a Pileup? | Center For Global Development*, Center for Global Development, https://www.cgdev.org/blog/2024-2025-replenishment-traffic-jam-are-we-headed-pileup (accessed on 11 June 2024). [12]

Kellerman, M. (2018), "The proliferation of multilateral development banks", *The Review of International Organizations*, Vol. 14/1, pp. 107-145, https://doi.org/10.1007/s11558-018-9302-y. [22]

Kenny, C. and S. Morris (2021), *A Climate-Dedicated Capital Increase at the World Bank and IFC*, Center for Global Development, https://www.cgdev.org/publication/climate-dedicated-capital-increase-world-bank-and-ifc. [11]

Kondoh Hisahiro (2024), "Emerging Donors on the Rise". [17]

MOPAN (2024), *Performance at a glance: World Health Organization (WHO)*, https://www.mopanonline.org/assessments/who2024/WHO%20Performance%20at%20a%20Glance_June_2024.pdf. [16]

OECD (2024), *Dashboard on DAC members' earmarked contributions to multilateral organisations*, https://oecd-main.shinyapps.io/DACearmarking/. [14]

OECD (2024), *From global to local: Multilateral actors and the pivot to locally led development*, https://one.oecd.org/document/DCD(2024)23/en/pdf?sessionId=1723453398474. [15]

OECD (2024), *Members' total use of the multilateral system*, http://data-explorer.oecd.org/s/s (accessed on 22 April 2024). [1]

OECD (2024), *Online profiles on DAC members' use of the multilateral system.* [13]

OECD (2022), *Multilateral Development Finance 2022*, OECD Publishing, Paris, https://doi.org/10.1787/9fea4cf2-en. [2]

OECD (2022), *States of Fragility 2022*, OECD Publishing, Paris, https://doi.org/10.1787/c7fedf5e-en. [8]

OECD (2020), *Multilateral Development Finance 2020*, OECD Publishing, Paris, https://doi.org/10.1787/e61fdf00-en. [3]

OECD (2015), *Multilateral Aid 2015: Better Partnerships for a Post-2015 World*, OECD Publishing, Paris, https://doi.org/10.1787/9789264235212-en. [5]

OECD/LEGAL/5019 (ed.) (2019), *DAC Recommendation on the Humanitarian-Development-Peace Nexus*, https://legalinstruments.oecd.org/public/doc/643/643.en.pdf. [9]

Reinsberg, B. and C. Siauwijaya (2024), "Does earmarked funding affect the performance of international organizations?", *Global Policy*, Vol. 15 (1), pp. 23-39, https://doi.org/10.1111/1758-5899.13270. [7]

UN General Assembly, E. (ed.) (2019), *UN Funding Compact*, https://unsdg.un.org/resources/implementation-general-assembly-resolution-71243-quadrennial-comprehensive-policy-review. [4]

UNSCEB (2024), *Financial Statistics*, https://unsceb.org/financial-statistics (accessed on 30 April 2024). [19]

Wang, H. (2019), "The New Development Bank and the Asian Infrastructure Investment Bank: China's Ambiguous Approach to Global Financial Governance", *Development and Change*, Vol. 50/1, pp. 221-244, https://doi.org/10.1111/dech.12473. [23]

World Bank Group (2024), *IDA - Contributor countries*, https://ida.worldbank.org/en/about/contributor-countries. [10]

World Bank Group (2024), *IDA20 Replenishment*, https://ida.worldbank.org/en/replenishments/ida20-replenishment. [20]

# 4 Financing from the multilateral system

The swift rebound and re-allocation of multilateral outflows observed in 2022 demonstrated the system's resilience and versatility, including its ability to pivot from one crisis to another. In response to recent calls for reform, MDBs are readily embracing new tasks and mandates, for example rapidly increasing climate-related development finance and private finance mobilisation. However, some cracks are appearing in the system as multilateral organisations are stretched thin in meeting a widening range of challenges and needs. Over time, efforts to increasingly leverage the system's resources lead to a rise in non-concessional finance, potentially affecting multilateral organisations' ability to target poverty and engage with countries facing public debt sustainability issues.

## Financing from the multilateral development system is resilient amidst multiple shocks and crises

### *Multilateral development outflows have nearly matched 2020's record levels*

**Multilateral outflows experienced a rebound in 2022, nearly reaching the record levels seen in 2020.** In 2022, multilateral outflows amounted to USD 259 billion, reflecting a 12% increase on the previous year (Figure 4.1). This recovery comes after a 12% decrease in 2021, when outflows were subdued following an exceptional expansion in financing to combat the COVID-19 crisis. The outflows in 2022 were not far behind the record level of USD 264 billion achieved in 2020. Of the total outflows in 2022, USD 46 billion (18%) were earmarked, while USD 213 billion (82%) were from multilateral organisations' core resources. As discussed in Chapter 3, a significant part of the increase in multilateral development finance between 2021 and 2022 can be attributed to heightened support for Ukraine.

#### Figure 4.1. Multilateral outflows in 2022 recovered from the previous year's temporary decline

Multilateral outflows (from core resources and earmarked), 2012-22

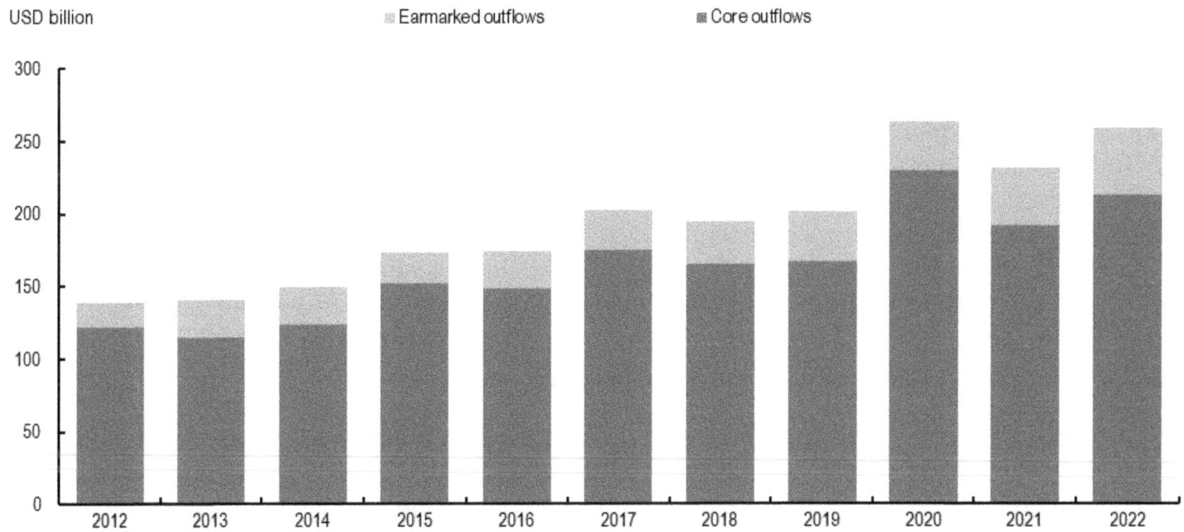


Note: Calculations are based on commitments, in 2022 constant prices.
Source: OECD (2024[11]), OECD Data Explorer, *Creditor Reporting System* (database), http://data-explorer.oecd.org/s/c.

### *The system increasingly relies on the leveraging capacity of multilateral development banks*

**Over the past decade, the increase in multilateral outflows has been primarily driven by the multilateral development banks, masking sluggish spending elsewhere**. Between 2012 and 2020, outflows from the World Bank Group and other MDBs rose substantially, by USD 35.3 billion and USD 61.8 billion respectively (Figure 4.2). In comparison, outflows from United Nations (UN) entities and vertical funds increased by a more modest USD 14.5 billion and USD 2.6 billion respectively over the same period.

**This picture is not matched by trends in multilateral inflows, implying that MDBs are stretching their leveraging capacity.** The surge in MDBs' outflows contrasts with the relatively flat trend of funding they receive from their members, presented in Chapter 3. This disparity underscores that MDBs' leveraging capacity is being stretched thin through the continued implementation of efficiency-focused measures aimed at optimising balance sheets.

**Figure 4.2. Outflows from the World Bank Group and other MDBs have increased most since 2012**

Multilateral outflows by type of multilateral organisation, 2012-22

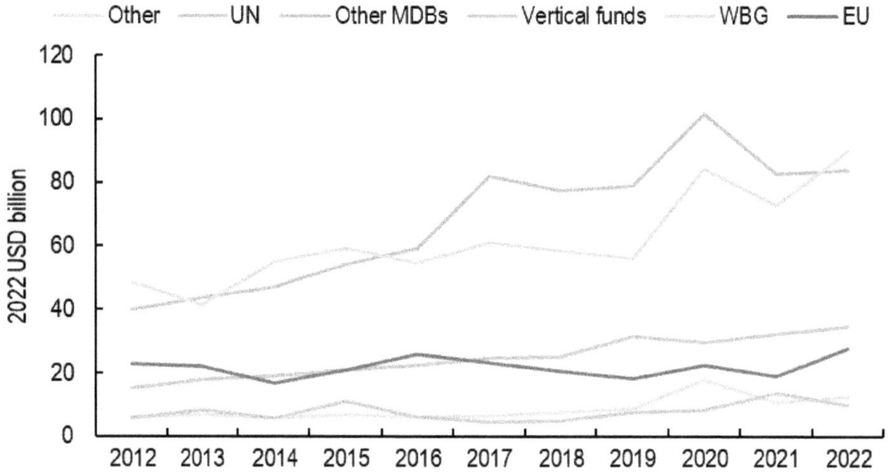


Note: Calculations are based on commitments, in 2022 constant prices.
Source: OECD (2024[1]), *Creditor Reporting System* (database), http://data-explorer.oecd.org/s/c.

**In 2022, the recovery of multilateral outflows was evident across most categories of organisations.** The European Union and the World Bank Group steeply increased their commitments in 2022, by 46% and 23% respectively. This contrasted with the more limited increases from UN entities (8%) and other MDBs (2%), and the 28% decrease registered by vertical funds. Notably, however, the decline in outflows from vertical funds follows a peak they reached in 2021. In absolute terms, the World Bank Group's increase of USD 17 billion accounted for 62% of the total 2022 increase in multilateral outflows.

### *Multilateral organisations' portfolios are versatile*

**Multilateral organisations' outflows are responsive to the financing needs generated by the global context.** The previous edition of this report stressed the ability of multilateral organisations, notably MDBs, to pivot their support towards health and social protection during the COVID-19 crisis, highlighting their flexibility and versatility (OECD, 2022[2]). Multilateral outflows targeting social sectors surged in 2020 and 2021 because of the COVID-19 pandemic, from 17% in 2019, to 24% in 2020 and 27% in 2021 (Figure 4.3). Meanwhile, outflows to infrastructure, which accounted for a quarter of multilateral outflows before the pandemic, receded to 20% from 2020. This capacity to adapt to changing circumstances was still evident in 2021 and 2022, this time driven by the need to help address the impact of Russia's war of aggression against Ukraine. For example, the share of the humanitarian sector in outflows increased from 7% in 2020, to 10% in 2021 and 13% in 2022. This reflects multilateral organisations' changing priorities as they shifted their focus from public health and social protection towards humanitarian crisis response.

## Figure 4.3. Multilateral organisations can adjust their sectoral allocations to respond to crises

Sectoral distribution of multilateral outflows (from core resources and earmarked), 2019-22

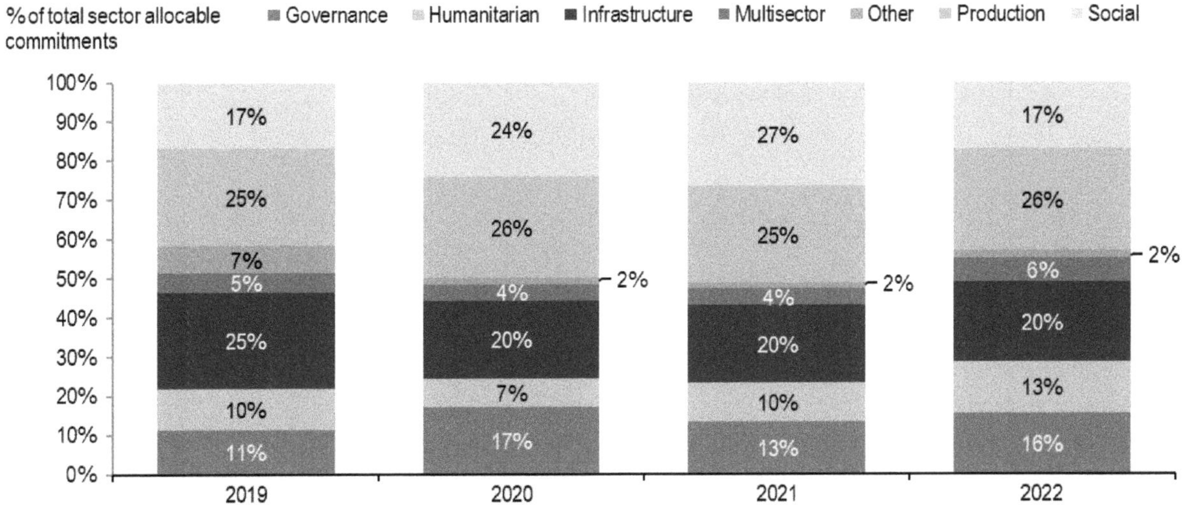


Note: Calculations are based on commitments, in 2022 constant prices.
Source: OECD (2024[1]), OECD Data Explorer, *Creditor Reporting System* (database), http://data-explorer.oecd.org/s/c.

**Budget support stood out for its versatility in helping countries weather budgetary issues created by various development challenges.** Between 2019 and 2020, multilateral outflows for budget support registered a significant rise – from 11% to 17% – as the multilateral development system supported developing countries during the first year of the COVID-19 pandemic. After decreasing to 13% in 2021, it increased again to 16% in 2022 as multilateral channels were used to offer budgetary relief to Ukraine.

**Specialised entities, such as the main vertical funds, also play a key role in helping the multilateral development system navigate from one crisis to another.** Financing from global health funds, for example, surged during the pandemic crises of Ebola in 2014-2015 and COVID-19 in 2020-2021. In fact, Figure 4.4 suggests that changes in vertical funds' outflows are better explained by the incidence of such crises rather than the timing of their replenishments. A potential cause for concern is that the release of exceptional amounts of financing to respond to ad hoc crises sometimes depletes resources needed to address the long-term challenges these vertical funds were originally created for. After the Ebola crisis, for instance, outflows from global health funds bottomed out and remained at pre-crisis levels for two consecutive years. In addition, recent health crises also appear to have diverted attention from other vertical funds' priorities, as evidenced by the dip in outflows from climate funds coinciding with peaks in global health funds' outflows during the Ebola and COVID-19 crises shown in the figure.

### Figure 4.4. Vertical funds allow the multilateral development system to pivot between crises

Outflows from climate and health-related vertical funds, 2012-22

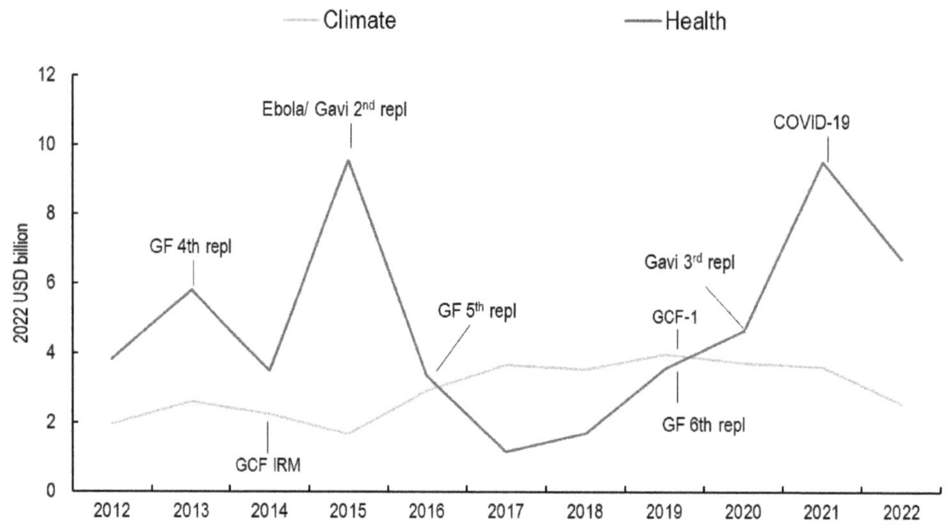


Note: Calculations are based on commitments, in 2022 constant prices. GCF: Green Climate Fund; GF: Global Fund to Fight AIDS, Tuberculosis and Malaria; IRM: initial resource mobilisation; Repl: replenishment.
Source: OECD (2024[11]), OECD Data Explorer, *Creditor Reporting System* (database), http://data-explorer.oecd.org/s/c.

**The system's ability to pivot between crises also resulted in declines in financing to other key development sectors.** The increase in multilateral finance for social sectors in 2020 and 2021 was driven by health investments for the COVID-19 response. Since 2020, however, financing to education, another key social sector, decreased significantly as response to successive crises was prioritised in multilateral outflows. Box 4.1 provides some insights on recent trends in multilateral finance for education, comparing it to the health sector, which has been successful at attracting multilateral investment.

### Box 4.1. Multilateral financing for education has been adversely affected by recent crises

**Multilateral finance for education decreased sharply, in contrast to recent increases in multilateral health finance.** Following a 34% increase between 2019 and 2020, multilateral finance for education declined for two consecutive years, reaching levels lower than those before the COVID-19 pandemic in 2022 (Figure 4.5). In contrast, multilateral finance for health soared by 95% in 2020 and 38% in 2021, remaining well above pre-COVID levels in 2022 despite a post-pandemic decline. This disparity reflects the greater attention given to the health sector due to its crucial role in addressing recent crises, such as the Ebola and COVID-19 pandemics.

**Figure 4.5. Social sectors have benefitted differently from recent crises**

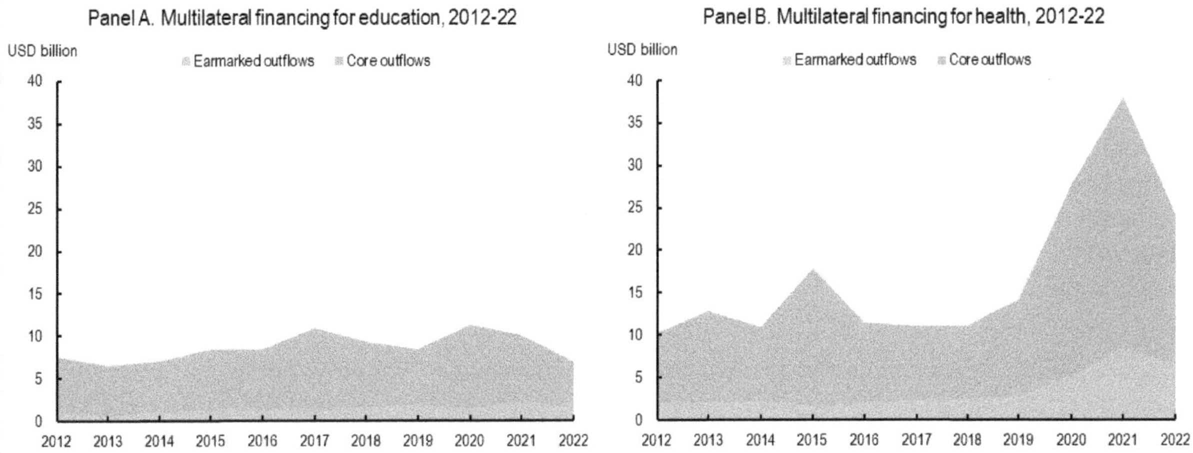


Note: Calculations are based on commitments in 2022 constant prices.
Source: OECD (2024[1]), OECD Data Explorer, *Creditor Reporting System* (database), http://data-explorer.oecd.org/s/c.

**The low levels of multilateral finance for education also reflect broader, structural challenges.** The decrease in multilateral finance for education observed in 2021 and 2022 is part of a wider trend of decreasing global aid to education. As successive crises have diverted attention from development sectors with long-term returns on investment, international aid to education declined by almost USD 2 billion, or 7%, between 2020 and 2021, from USD 19.3 billion to USD 17.8 billion. Furthermore, the gap between commitments and disbursements in multilateral finance for education is larger than in other sectors. According to Education Finance Watch, an average USD 1.7 billion in education aid from multilateral sources has gone unspent annually since 2017 (Bend et al., 2023[3]).

**As well as shifting the sectoral allocation of their outflows, multilateral organisations have also demonstrated a remarkable ability to embrace new priorities swiftly.** The next section explores two areas where this adaptability is evident: private finance mobilisation and climate-related development finance.

## The system is venturing beyond traditional mandates to tackle cutting-edge development challenges

**Alongside their traditional mandates, multilateral organisations are stepping up efforts to take on new priorities in financing the sustainable development agenda.** This section delves into the evolving role of multilateral organisations over the past decade in the realms of private finance mobilisation (Section 4.2.1) as well as climate and biodiversity-related development finance (Section 4.2.2), highlighting the notable progress achieved in both areas. Yet, in both cases, substantial additional efforts are required to achieve the transformative change needed to meet the ambitions of the global development agenda.

### Mobilising private finance is now a key focus of multilateral efforts, although results have been slow to materialise

#### *Multilateral providers lead efforts to mobilise private finance*

**In 2022, multilateral providers mobilised USD 47 billion in private finance, compared to 14 USD billion mobilised by DAC members** and their development finance institutions (Figure 4.6). The share of multilateral actors in total amounts mobilised increased from 67% in 2015 to 77% in 2022. However, this does not take into account the amounts mobilised by domestic public development banks in developing and emerging countries, such as the Development Bank of Southern Africa (DBSA) and the Brazilian Development Bank (BNDES), which play crucial roles in catalysing private investment in their regional and local economies.

**Figure 4.6. Multilateral organisations have driven the increase in private finance mobilisation**

Private finance mobilised, 2013-22

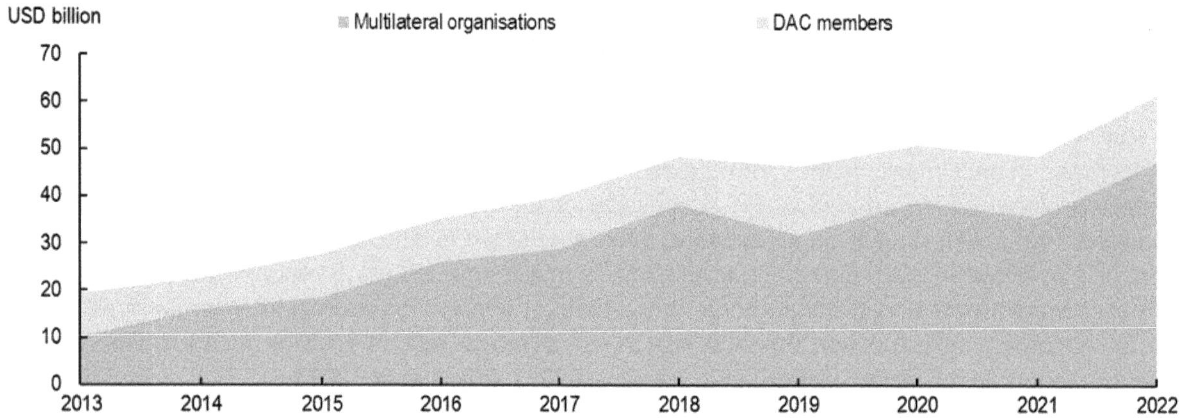


Note: Calculations are based on 2022 current prices, as inflation-adjusted constant price data are not available.
Source: OECD (2024[4]), OECD Data Explorer, *Mobilised private finance for development* (database), http://data-explorer.oecd.org/s/q

**The recent increase in multilateral mobilisation of private finance is driven by a few major players.** Among multilateral organisations, private finance mobilisation is primarily led by the MDBs and EU institutions. Between 2020 and 2022, the International Finance Corporation (IFC), Inter-American Development Bank (IADB), the Multilateral Investment Guarantee Agency (MIGA) and the EU institutions mobilised the largest amounts of private finance. Some vertical funds were also effective in mobilising private finance for specific purposes. For instance, the Green Climate Fund (GCF) has emerged as a significant new player in this field, mobilising USD 1.8 billion in 2022. In recent years, IFC and IADB were the only multilateral organisations to substantially increase mobilisation amounts, albeit from fairly low levels in 2020 and 2021 when the pandemic-induced global recession affected private investments. IFC doubled its mobilised amounts over this period, from USD 8.6 billion in 2020 to over USD 20 billion in 2022. With a private-sector mandate, a broad investor network, and extensive experience in building scalable syndication platforms – such as the Managed Co-Lending Portfolio Program (MCPP) (Box 4.2) – IFC has a distinct comparative advantage. Similarly, the amounts mobilised by IADB rose from USD 3.8 billion in 2020 to USD 7.9 billion in 2022, representing a 109% increase. IADB's private sector arm, IDB Invest, in particular, has expanded its mobilisation through innovative products such as the B-Bond (Box 4.2). On the other hand, mobilisation by other multilateral organisations remained relatively stagnant or declined in 2022. For example, the amounts mobilised by the African Development Bank (AfDB) fell from a peak of

USD 9.2 billion in 2020 to USD 2.2 billion in 2022, although it should be noted that the 2020 peak was mainly due to a large-scale infrastructure project in Mozambique (OECD, 2023[5]).

## Box 4.2. Tapping into institutional investor pools to increase MDBs' mobilisation performance

Over the past decade, MDBs have developed new programs and products that enable them to extend their reach and engage with new actors. Using innovative approaches, MDBs can mobilise finance from institutional investors such as insurance companies and pension funds, which due to regulatory restrictions, cannot directly invest in developing country loans. By tapping into new investor pools, MDBs can therefore effectively scale up amounts of finance mobilised. This box highlights two examples: IFC's Managed Co-Lending Portfolio Program (MCPP) and IDB Invest's B Bond.

### IFC's Managed Co-Lending Portfolio Program (MCPP)

MCPP provides a platform for institutional investors such as asset management and insurance companies to participate in IFC's investments in developing countries. Investors set loan eligibility criteria and portfolio concentration limits in an upfront agreement with IFC. Investors pledge capital, and IFC deploys their funds into loans that are selected based on the pre-agreed eligibility criteria, alongside IFC's own funds and on the same terms. Project appraisal, approval, commitment, and supervision are delegated to IFC, thus limiting origination and portfolio management costs for participating investors. Since MCPP's launch in 2013, IFC has raised over USD 16 billion from 17 institutional investors and global credit insurance companies.

### IDB Invest's B Bond

The B Bond is a financial instrument that allows IDB Invest to reach a broader investor base by including firms that can only invest in securities, and not in regular loans. The loan agreement with the borrower is structured similarly to a standard A/B loan, where IDB Invest, as the lender of record, administering the entire loan, retains a portion of the loan for its own account (the "A Loan") and sells participations in the remaining portion to eligible private lenders (the "B Loan"). However, in the case of the B Bond, the B loan participant is a special purpose vehicle that raises funds by issuing securities (B Bonds) through private placement formats, which are sold to institutional investors. The B Bond structure has been especially successful in attracting private investors to Uruguay's renewable energy sector.

Source: MDB Task Force on Mobilization (2024[6]), *Mobilization of Private Finance by Multilateral Development Banks and Development Finance Institutions in 2022*, https://www.ifc.org/content/dam/ifc/doc/2024/2022-joint-report-mobilization-of-private-finance-by-mdbs-dfis.pdf.

**Multilateral providers use a diverse array of leveraging mechanisms to mobilise private finance, with a noticeable division of roles among them.** MIGA, being a guarantee agency, uses guarantees exclusively (Figure 4.7), while other multilateral organisations use a mix of mechanisms. For instance, IFC primarily engages in direct investment in companies and special purpose vehicles[1] (SPVs), which accounted for 62% of its activities in 2022. It also uses a smaller share of syndicated loans[2] (14%) and guarantees (19%). IADB, on the other hand, has predominantly increased its mobilisation through syndicated loans, which accounted for 63% of its mobilisation activities in 2022. In comparison, EU institutions, including the European Investment Bank (EIB), mainly use credit lines[3] to financial intermediaries (47%) and investments in collective investment vehicles (CIVs) (29%). The relatively newer player GCF primarily focuses on investments in CIVs.

**Figure 4.7. Multilateral organisations use a diverse range of instruments to mobilise private finance**

Private finance mobilised by multilateral provider, 2020-22

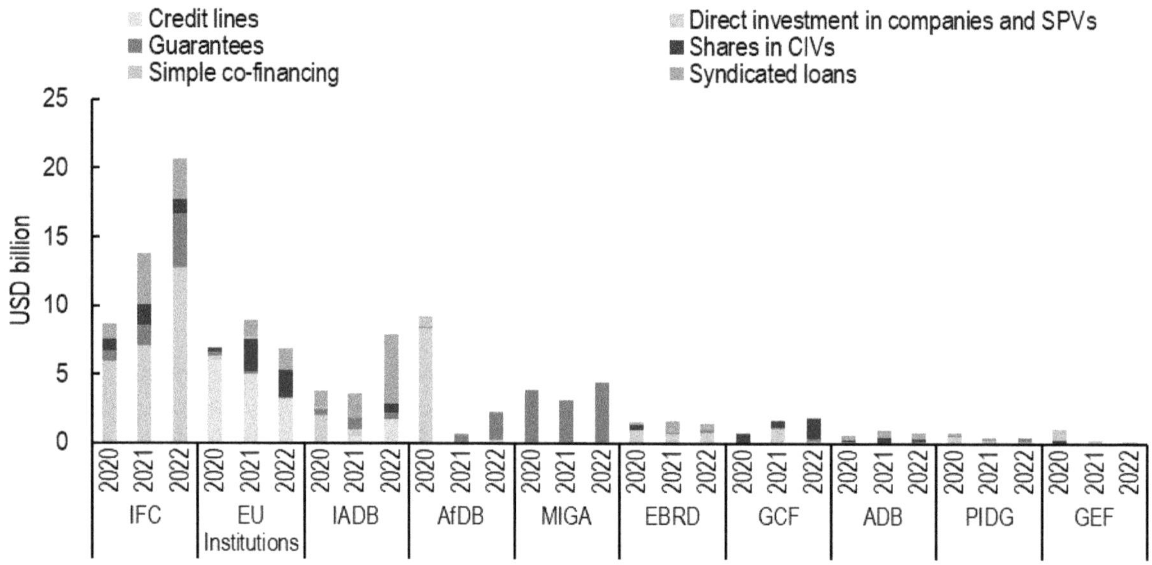


Note: Calculations are based on 2022 current prices, as inflation-adjusted constant price data are not available. ADB: Asian Development Bank; AfDB: African Development Bank; CIV: collective investment vehicle; EBRD: European Bank for Reconstruction and Development; GCF: Green Climate Fund; GEF: Global Environment Facility; IADB: Inter-American Development Bank; IFC: International Finance Corporation; MIGA: Multilateral Investment Guarantee Agency; PIDG: Private Infrastructure Development Group; SPV: special purpose vehicle.
Source: OECD (2024[1]), OECD Data Explorer, *Mobilised private finance for development* (database), http://data-explorer.oecd.org/s/q.

**Of the various instruments used to mobilise finance, guarantees are garnering increased attention for their significant potential.** Several studies have highlighted the mobilisation potential of guarantees (Garbacz, Vilalta and Moller, 2021[7]) (Convergence, 2019[8]) (Humphrey and Prizzon, 2014[9]). For instance, the G20 Independent Expert Group report on Strengthening Multilateral Development Banks advocated for an expanded use of guarantees to mitigate risk and catalyse private finance (G20 IEG, 2023[10]). Similarly, the Independent High-Level Expert Group on Climate Finance called on MDBs to revamp and bolster their guarantee programmes (Bhattacharya et al., 2023[11]). In response to these calls, several multilateral organisations have recently launched initiatives to create new guarantee programmes and platforms and to strengthen existing ones (Box 4.3).

### Box 4.3. Enhanced guarantee schemes at the World Bank and in the European Union

The World Bank Group and the European Fund for Sustainable Development Plus (EFSD+) offer two examples of concrete steps taken by multilateral organisations to enhance their guarantee schemes. These efforts aim to increase their capacity to mobilise private finance to support sustainable development projects.

#### A one-stop shop for World Bank Group guarantees

The World Bank Group is in the process of overhauling its guarantee programmes to streamline process and achieve greater impact. Starting in July 2024, a one-stop shop housed at MIGA will consolidate the 20 guarantee products that were previously spread across the institution. This platform will feature a simplified and comprehensive product menu, as well as a common approach for all guarantee reviews, eliminating redundancies while enhancing transparency and accessibility to clients. The initiative also seeks to triple the WBG's annual guarantee issuance to USD 20 billion by 2030 by focusing resources on high-impact projects and portfolios and offering new and innovative guarantee products.

#### The European Fund for Sustainable Development Plus (EFSD+)

The EFSD+ is one of the financing tools of Global Gateway, the EU's new strategy to promote sustainable investment in the European Union's partner countries. Offering a variety of risk-sharing instruments totalling up to EUR 40 billion, the EFSD+ aims to mobilise up to EUR 135 billion of public and private financing to help partner countries achieve the Sustainable Development Goals (SDGs). The EFSD+ Guarantee is deployed via a range of eligible development finance institutions, notably the EIB, which act as the EU's implementation partners on the ground.

Source: World Bank Group (2024[12]), *World Bank Group Prepares Major Overhaul to Guarantee Business*, https://www.worldbank.org/en/news/press-release/2024/02/27/world-bank-group-prepares-major-overhaul-to-guarantee-business; European Commission (2024[13]), *European Fund for Sustainable Development Plus*, https://international-partnerships.ec.europa.eu/funding-and-technical-assistance/funding-instruments/european-fund-sustainable-development-plus_en

### *Delivering on Agenda 2030 will require strengthening the mobilisation capacity of multilateral organisations*

**Despite significant progress, multilateral organisations face mounting pressure to enhance their efforts to mobilise more finance.** The total amount mobilised in 2022, USD 62 billion, is still far short of the G20 Independent Expert Group's target of USD 240 billion by 2030 (G20 IEG, 2023[10]). In addition, existing mechanisms have demonstrated their limitations in rapidly scaling up private finance. In response to these challenges, many MDBs have made private sector finance a central focus of their ongoing reforms. For example, in 2023, the World Bank Group launched the Private Sector Investment Lab, a collaborative initiative with the chief executive officers of leading global private sector institutions aimed at developing specific scalable approaches for mobilising private capital more effectively (World Bank, 2023[14]). Furthermore, during its Annual Meetings in May 2024, the AfDB announced a five-point programme to accelerate investments in Africa. As part of this initiative, the organisation plans to overhaul its operational business and embrace a greater risk appetite to scale up its financing to the private sector, with the goal of tripling its non-sovereign financing operations to USD 7.5 billion annually over the next decade (African Development Bank Group, 2024[15]).

**Although there have been advances in increasing private finance for the countries most in need, many remain at risk of being left behind in the mobilisation agenda.** In 2021-22, the share of private finance mobilised for least developed countries and other low-income countries (LDCs and other LICs) remained fairly low at 8%, though this was an improvement on 4% in 2016-17 (Figure 4.8). Investment challenges in LDCs stem from national-level factors, including political instability and high indebtedness, as well as project-level risks such as high project preparation costs (Lundsgaarde, 2023[16]). This underscores the importance of creating an enabling environment for private sector development, without which mobilisation performance in the poorest and most vulnerable countries is likely to remain limited.

**Figure 4.8. Only a small amount of private finance is mobilised in least developed countries**

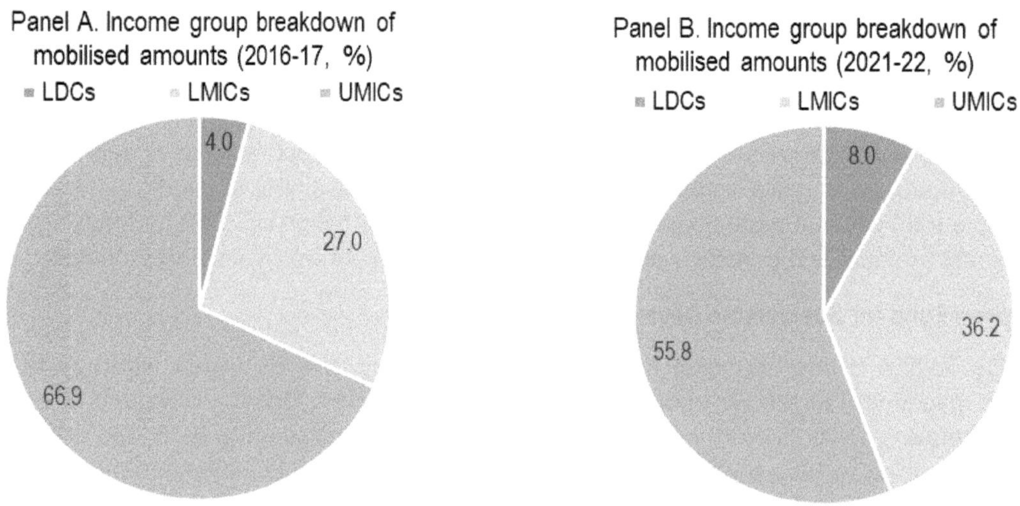


Note: Calculations are based on 2022 current prices, as inflation-adjusted constant price data are not available. LDCs: least developed countries and other low-income countries; LMICs: lower-middle income countries; UMICs: upper-middle income countries.
Source: OECD (2024[1]), OECD Data Explorer, *Mobilised private finance for development* (database), http://data-explorer.oecd.org/s/c.

**Efforts aimed at boosting private finance mobilisation in the most challenging contexts have also produced mixed results.** Multilateral organisations have implemented measures to facilitate private finance in these environments, including through initiatives such as the IDA Private Sector Window (Box 4.4). However, concerns have emerged about the slow pace of results from some of these initiatives, and doubts about the value for money and additionality of interventions that use scarce concessional resources to subsidise private investments. This situation calls for clear criteria to explicitly and consciously evaluate the benefits and costs of designing blended finance initiatives, especially in least developed countries and other challenging contexts.

### Box 4.4. IDA's Private Sector Window can improve its additionality and transparency

**IDA's Private Sector Window (PSW), approved in 2016, aims to scale up private investments in IDA-eligible, i.e. low-income countries.** The PSW, introduced as part of the IDA18 replenishment, provides risk mitigation through four facilities for projects undertaken by IFC and MIGA: (1) project-based guarantees to crowd in private investment in large infrastructure projects; (2) cover for MIGA guarantees through first-loss and risk participation; (3) long-term local currency hedging solutions; and (4) blended finance solutions to increase SME finance among other sectors.

**The PSW got off to a slow start, using only half of its initial envelope.** It received an initial allocation of 1.8 billion in special drawing rights (SDR) (approximately USD 2.5 billion) as part of IDA18, followed by an additional USD 1.68 billion for IDA 19 and USD 2.5 billion for IDA 20. Under IDA18, however, only 55% of PSW funds were approved for investment, leaving nearly half of its enveloped unused. More recently, the pace of project approvals has picked up as the capacity of IFC and MIGA to develop transactions using PSW subsidies grows over time. The PSW is now expected to commit all allocated funds (USD 5.5 billion) by the end of IDA20 (June 2025).

**The PSW has room for improvement in several key areas.** According to a recent assessment by Mathiasen et al. (2024[17]), the performance of the PSW has been mixed. Some evidence suggests that PSW projects tend to have higher development impact than non-PSW supported projects and permit IFC engagement with riskier counterparties. However, there are doubts about the additionality of the PSW. For example, IFC and MIGA commitments in IDA-eligible countries that are not supported by PSW are decreasing. The mobilisation effect of PSW is also questionable, with less private finance mobilised in PSW-supported than in non-PSW supported projects. Moreover, many PSW transactions have subsidised short-term trade and working capital finance, which typically has limited impact on long-term market development. Critics have also noted the opaque nature of project selection and the lack of competitive bidding.

Source: Mathiasen et al. (2024[17]), *IDA 21 and the Private Sector Window*, https://www.cgdev.org/sites/default/files/ida-21-and-private-sector-window.pdf.

## *Climate-related multilateral development finance is growing, but more is needed*

### *The climate related share of multilateral outflows is increasing, driven especially by a surge in MDB financing*

**Multilateral organisations, particularly MDBs, are increasingly embracing climate action in their mandates.** As discussed in Chapter 2, expanding mandates to address global challenges is one area of the MDB reform agenda where notable progress has been made. Most MDBs have already incorporated global public goods into their mandates and in their country diagnostics and strategies.

**The climate finance architecture encompasses a large and growing variety of multilateral entities.** MDBs play key roles in climate action, leveraging their financial firepower. Among the climate funds, only the Green Climate Fund (GCF) comes close to the level of financing provided by the main MDBs (Figure 4.9). The volume of climate finance provided by multilateral institutions does not necessarily correlate with their age. Notably, the relatively new IMF Resilience and Sustainability Trust (RST) has already committed over USD 1 billion between 2020 and 2022, surpassing older funding mechanisms such as the Adaptation Fund and the Climate Investment Funds (CIFs). Multilateral organisations have also become significant providers of biodiversity-related development finance, accounting for around 30% of total development finance for biodiversity from a range of actors (e.g. DAC members, South-South and triangular co-operation providers, philanthropies and other private actors) over 2015-2022 (see Box 4.5).

**Figure 4.9. Among the green funds, only the Green Climate Fund approaches MDBs' financial capacity**

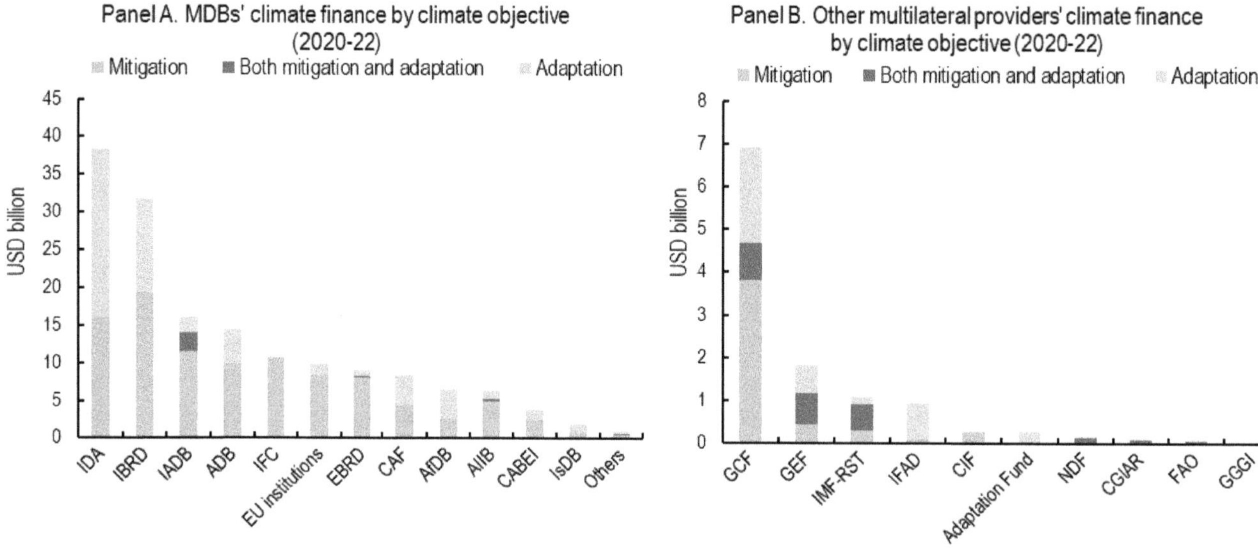


Note: Calculations are based on climate components of MDB commitments, in 2022 constant prices. ADB: Asian Development Bank; AfDB: African Development Bank; AIIB: Asian Infrastructure Investment Bank; CABEI: Central American Bank for Economic Integration; CAF: Development Bank of Latin America and the Caribbean; CGIAR: Consultative Group on International Agricultural Research; CIF: Climate Investment Funds; EBRD: European Bank for Reconstruction and Development; FAO: Food and Agriculture Organization of the United Nations; GCF: Green Climate Fund; GEF: Global Environment Facility; GGGI: Global Green Growth Institute; IADB: Inter-American Development Bank; IBRD: International Bank for Reconstruction and Development; IDA: International Development Association; IFAD: International Fund for Agricultural Development; IFC: International Finance Corporation; IMF-RST: International Monetary Fund – Resilience and Sustainability Trust; ISDB: Islamic Development Bank; NDF: Nordic Development Fund.
Source: OECD (2024[18]), Climate-related development finance at the activity level: Recipient perspective (database), https://www.oecd.org/development/financing-sustainable-development/development-finance-topics/climate-change.htm.

**Box 4.5. Multilateral development providers' contributions to biodiversity have increased significantly**

Contributions from multilateral organisations represent about 30% of total development finance for biodiversity[1] and the sustainable use of natural resources. Indeed, multilateral biodiversity-related development finance (both concessional and non-concessional) increased significantly over 2015-2022, reaching USD 5.7 -11.3 billion in 2022, depending on the approach considered[2]. However, the relative share of biodiversity-related activities out of the total multilateral development finance portfolio remained low (2%-3% on average over the period) and would need to increase for these institutions to contribute meaningfully to the Kunming-Montreal Global Biodiversity Framework (KMGBF).

MDBs account for 71% of total multilateral biodiversity-related development finance over 2015-22. In turn, other environmental funds and organisations that are part of the United Nations system account for 22% and 7%, respectively. The top recipients include China, Colombia, Mexico, Indonesia and Brazil, with most of the multilateral biodiversity-related development finance flows targeting UMICs (50%), followed by LMICs (26%), and LDCs and other lower-income countries LICs (24%). The region that received most biodiversity-related development finance from multilateral institutions over 2015-22 was Asia, followed by Latin American and the Caribbean and Africa. Overall, multilateral biodiversity-related finance was mainly deployed through loans (70%) followed by grants (28%). This contrasts with how biodiversity-related development finance is provided by bilateral donors, 68% of which was provided in the form of grants between 2015-22.

Most of the estimated multilateral biodiversity-related development finance is allocated to three sectors: agriculture (22%), general environment protection (16%), and water (13%, including water supply and sanitation). In some sectors, the estimates show that biodiversity-related finance can be highly integrated into multilateral investments, notably forestry (64%), general environment protection (50%, of which 41% was destined to biodiversity interventions) or fishing (37%). However, none of the sectors had biodiversity-related objectives as a main driver for multilateral investments. In effect, multilateral institutions, and in particular MDBs, have committed to step up action to further mainstream nature into their policies and operations, as well as to develop methodologies to track and report 'nature positive' investments.

Note: 1. Development finance for biodiversity refers to ODA and other official flows (OOF) that contribute to the conservation, restoration and sustainable use of biodiversity. 2. The analysis reflects two approaches: biodiversity-related, which reflects the full values of flows reported to the OECD; and biodiversity-specific, which considers a coefficient for activities targeting biodiversity as a secondary objective. For more information on the methodology used, see Annex A of OECD (forthcoming[19]).
Source: OECD (forthcoming[19]), Biodiversity and Development Finance 2015-2022: Contributing to Target 19 of the Kunming-Montreal Global Biodiversity Framework.

**In the past decade, the role of MDBs in climate-related development finance[4] has significantly increased, as evidenced by the growing share of their operations that includes a climate component.** MDBs' climate-related development finance surged by nearly 300% between 2013 and 2022, from USD 16.4 billion to USD 65.2 billion (Figure 4.10, Panel A).[5] In addition, MDBs have increased the share of their total operations dedicated to climate. In 2015, climate-related development finance constituted about 15% of MDBs' total operations, compared to 24% in 2022 (Mitchell and Wickstead, 2024[20]).

## Figure 4.10. MDBs' climate-related development finance has increased and adaptation represents a growing share

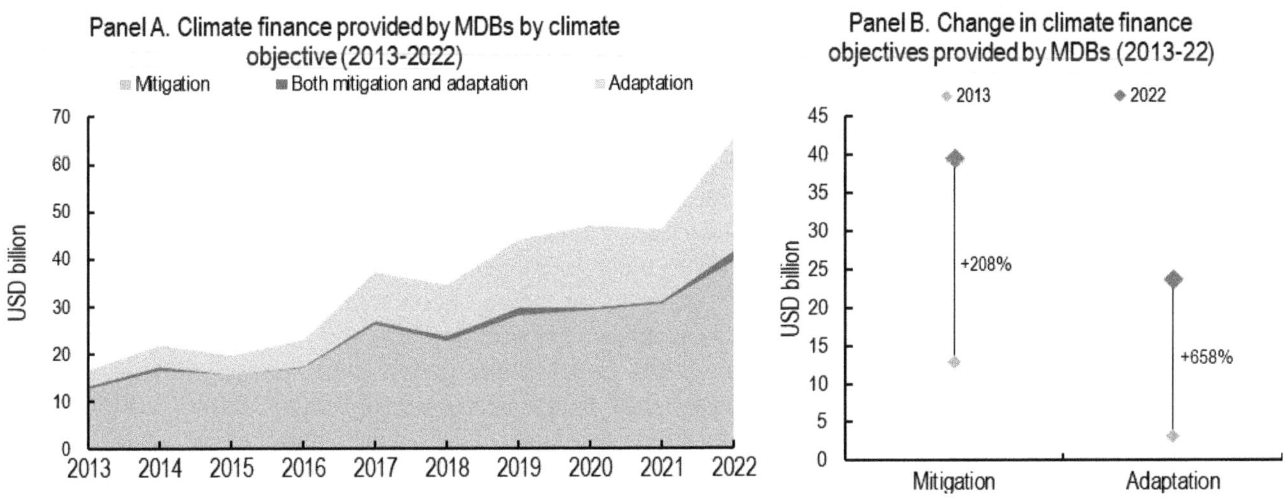


Note: Calculations are based on climate components of MDB commitments, in 2022 constant prices. MDBs included are the ones noted in Figure 4.9 Panel A.
Source: OECD (2024[18]), *Climate-related development finance at the activity level: Recipient perspective* (database), https://www.oecd.org/development/financing-sustainable-development/development-finance-topics/climate-change.htm.

**MDBs are increasingly taking a lead role in adaptation.** In 2022, MDBs allocated a total of USD 23 billion for adaptation. This focus on adaptation emerged in the early years of the last decade and has since represented an increasing portion of MDBs' overall climate commitments (Figure 4.10, Panel A). While adaptation-focused projects accounted for only 19% of MDBs' climate commitments in 2013, this proportion had nearly doubled, to 36%, by 2022. This shift was driven by a remarkable 658% surge in adaptation-related development finance between 2013 and 2022, compared to a 208% increase in mitigation (Figure 4.10, Panel B). IDA and IBRD stand out in particular, dedicating approximately half of their climate commitments to adaptation-related projects (59% and 39% respectively) between 2020 and 2022, while most other MDBs remained primarily focused on mitigation.

**While the surge in MDBs' climate action is positive, there are concerns about the rigour and quality of the climate reporting in development finance.** As development finance providers, including MDBs, are under immense public pressure to deliver on climate commitments, there can be incentives to inflate climate finance figures. In light of this "greenwashing" risk, there are calls to improve the climate reporting by introducing standardised methodologies that clearly explain and justify how a project contributes to climate change mitigation or adaptation (Farr, Morrissey and Donaldson, 2022[21]) (Núñez-Mujica, Ramachandran and Morris, 2023[22]).

### Changes to multilateral organisations' models are required to enhance support to the climate agenda

**A step change in the volume of climate-related development finance provided by the multilateral development system is urgently needed to address the climate crisis effectively.** While the rise in multilateral climate-related development finance up to 2022 is commendable, it is widely acknowledged that current levels are still insufficient. The United Nations Framework Convention on Climate Change's recent analysis of financing needs notes that developing countries require at least USD 6 trillion by 2030 to implement less than half of their existing Nationally Determined Contributions (UNFCCC Standing Committee on Finance, 2021[23]). In 2023, at COP28, ten MDBs joined forces to issue an ambitious joint statement and a forward-looking vision to accelerate climate action (COP28, 2023[24]). Among their pledges was a commitment to triple climate finance, aiming to reach USD 180 billion in additional commitments through multi-year programmes in the next decade.

**Another issue is the disparities in the allocation of funds, with insufficient resources directed towards the most vulnerable and high-impact areas, such as adaptation efforts in low-income countries**. The targeting of the poorest countries in multilateral climate action has improved but could still be enhanced through an increased focus on adaptation. The share of MDBs' climate-related development finance directed towards LDCs and other LICs has grown, largely due to a greater emphasis on adaptation, but the overall volume remains modest. Between 2020 and 2022, MDBs allocated 20% of their climate finance to LDCs and other LICs, a 4% increase from the 16% allocated during 2017-2019. However, this remains lower than the 35% directed to LMICs and 31% to UMICs. The rise in climate-related development finance for LDCs and LICs was primarily driven by an increased focus on adaptation, which constitutes a significant portion of the finance directed towards lower-income economies (European Investment Bank, 2023[25]). In 2022, 61% of climate-related development finance for LDCs and other LICs was dedicated to adaptation, compared to 39% for LMICs and 29% for UMICs (Figure 4.11). Once operational, the World Bank-hosted Loss and Damage Fund, established to assist developing countries that are particularly vulnerable to the adverse effects of climate change, will likely increase multilateral climate-related finance and further shift its allocations towards lower-income countries.

## Figure 4.11. MDBs' climate finance mainly targets mitigation-relevant sectors despite an increase in the share of adaptation finance

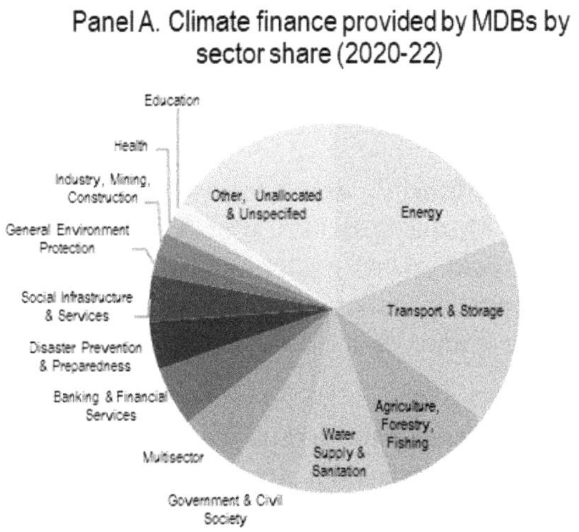


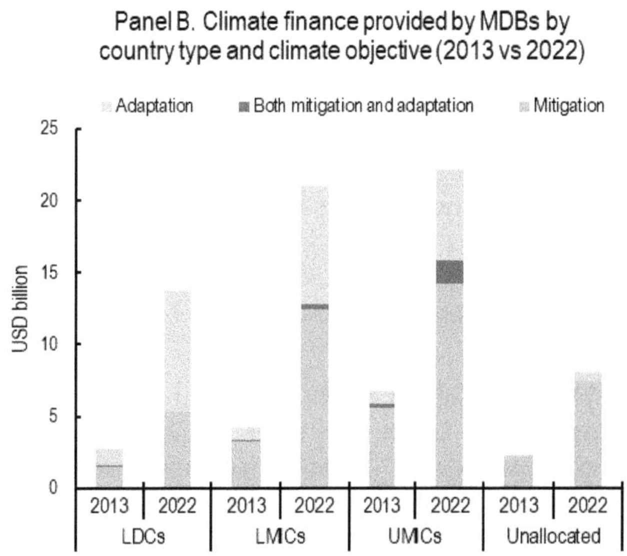


Note: Calculations are based on climate components of MDB commitments, in 2022 constant prices. LDCs: least developed countries and other low-income countries; LMICs: lower-middle income countries; UMICs: upper-middle income countries.
Source: OECD (2024[18]), *Climate-related development finance at the activity level: Recipient perspective* (database), https://www.oecd.org/development/financing-sustainable-development/development-finance-topics/climate-change.htm.

**Most of the climate-related development finance provided by MDBs is channeled through loans, with a large share directed towards mitigation projects in the infrastructure and production sectors.** Between 2020 and 2022, over three-quarters of MDBs' climate-related development finance was channeled through debt instruments. The largest share of this finance was allocated to mitigation efforts in the energy, transport and storage, agriculture, forestry, fishing, and water supply and sanitation sectors. This allocation highlights that much remains to be done to achieve the goal of multiplying the volume of adaptation finance set in the COP28.

**Critical gaps must still be closed for multilateral organisations to deliver on their ambitious climate finance objectives.** Recent research by MOPAN examined the readiness and positioning of MDBs to deliver on their COP28 Joint Statement (MOPAN, 2024[26]). Building upon evidence from MOPAN assessments of eight MDBs (the World Bank, IFC, EBRD, AfDB, ADB, IADB, IDB Invest and IFAD), the study highlighted the deficiencies in these institutions' business models that need to be fixed for them to effectively meet their COP28 ambitions (Box 4.6).

### Box 4.6. Filling the significant gaps in MDBs' business models and support for climate change

**Despite the progress made over the last decade, MDBs are not yet fully positioned to deliver on their COP28 commitments.** Recent MOPAN assessments have highlighted achievements in scaling up climate finance, strengthening expertise and human resources, as well as identifying new and innovative instruments. However, MDBs continue to demonstrate gaps in their business models and support to climate change that could hinder their ability to deliver on their COP28 ambitions.

**MDB knowledge and policy advice are crucial for promoting an enabling environment for climate action, yet their ability to demonstrate well-co-ordinated contribution to critical policy shifts remains limited.** MOPAN (2024[26]) points out inefficiencies due to insufficient co-ordination. For example, climate-related analytical work is often delivered in a fragmented way by MDBs, with multiple MDBs addressing the same issues in the same countries. Additionally, knowledge work is rarely reflected in country strategy results frameworks, and results measurement is often confined to output-focused indicators, limiting the ability to assess real impact.

**MDBs are not systematically employing "whole-of-institution" approaches that foster an enabling environment for private sector climate action.** Most MDBs lack specific guidelines and mechanisms for promoting collaboration between the public and private sector in pipeline and project development. This results in a fundamental mismatch between operational processes and incentives underlying public and private sector operations, with private sector operations requiring a more agile approach.

**The channelling of concessional finance through donor trust funds remains inadequate and inefficient.** Donor trust funds are fragmented across numerous individual single-donor partnerships and mechanisms, leading to high transaction costs and reporting burdens. Efforts to consolidate these funds into multi-donor or "umbrella" funds have yielded important efficiencies. However, for these efficiencies to be realised, donors must be willing to accept trade-offs in terms of control and visibility for the sake of greater overall efficiency.

**Reporting on climate results will require substantial changes to MDBs' project selection and results architecture.** Climate finance is often fragmented across projects that may have limited tangible linkages to climate outcomes. The current emphasis on aggregating climate finance ex-ante has reduced the incentive to identify and track tangible climate outcomes for projects and country strategies ex-post. At the institutional level, MDB corporate climate indicators remain highly fragmented. Although MDBs have committed to harmonising their corporate results frameworks, these issues point to important gaps throughout the climate results architecture that cannot be resolved by changes in corporate indicators alone. Instead, comprehensive reforms are needed to ensure that climate results are effectively measured and reported.

**Addressing remaining gaps in MDBs' operational guidelines, processes and incentives could enable them to better work as a system through country-led platforms.** Significant shortcomings in these areas currently impede closer collaboration, for example in initiatives such as Just Energy Transition Partnerships (JETPs). In particular, when resources or in-country presence are limited, co-ordination with partners receives less emphasis. In addition, MOPAN's research underscored that joint monitoring and knowledge work across development partners remain limited.

Note: MOPAN's analysis reflects on the readiness and positioning of MDBs to deliver on their COP28 Joint Statement. It builds upon evidence from MOPAN Assessments of eight MDBs (the World Bank, IFC, EBRD, AfDB, ADB, IADB, IDB Invest and IFAD) complemented by a literature review, consultations with stakeholders and a review of 40 MDB Country Strategies.
Source: MOPAN (2024[26]), *Accelerating Climate Action: Multilateral Development Banks' Readiness and Performance*.

As multilateral organisations adapt their missions, operations and financial models to address new priorities on the multilateral agenda, such as private finance mobilisation and climate finance, concerns are also being voiced around their ability to continue delivering on more traditional long-term development goals (Elgar et al., 2023[27]). Alongside bilateral donors, multilateral organisations need to balance country-driven demands for assistance with growing needs to address global challenges. The next section explores this trade-off in greater detail.

## Multilateral organisations are torn between their traditional roles and new mandates and responsibilities

**Multilateral organisations face a growing tension between the traditional focus on long-term development, and the urgent need to scale up their contributions to global public goods and crisis response.** Ongoing multilateral reform initiatives call for a revision of their mandates to reinforce their role as providers of global public goods (Chapter 2). Simultaneously, multiple global crises – including the pandemic, climate change, Russia's war of aggression on Ukraine, and the Israel-Hamas conflict – have interconnected in ways that are significant in scope and devastating in effect. Multilateral organisations now face mounting expectations to pivot their support to address the impacts of these crises. However, responding to the escalating demand for crisis response often involves diverting ODA away from development efforts, creating a cyclical pattern that perpetuates crisis, conflict and fragility, while detracting from traditional multilateral mandates, which revolve around long-term development, with poverty reduction taking a central place. The following sections explore the extent to which multilateral development finance aligns with the goal of reducing poverty (Section 4.3.1), and how current trends may affect this relationship in the future (Section 4.3.2).

### *The multilateral development system's capacity to address poverty mainly relies on its concessional, donor-funded facilities*

**The fight against poverty has historically been a central focus of concessional multilateral development finance.** Many multilateral organisations have mandates dedicated to poverty reduction, leveraging their ability to provide concessional finance to the poorest or most vulnerable countries. They also support key sectors related to poverty alleviation, such as social protection, health and education. Donor contributions are essential to the financing model of these institutions, allowing them to offer support through grants or concessional loans. Examples of such institutions include the concessional windows of MDBs, UNDS entities and vertical funds.

**Although there is still room for improvement, multilateral organisations' outflows display a stronger focus on poverty than bilateral development finance**. Figure 1.10 illustrates the correlation between the commitments of bilateral and multilateral donors and the poverty headcount ratio of recipient countries. It suggests that multilateral organisations are able to target poverty through their concessional finance, while bilateral providers' flows – whether concessional or not – have almost no[6] correlation with the poverty levels of recipient countries. Bilateral funds earmarked through multilateral organisations, which are typically provided on concessional terms, show a positive correlation with poverty, although it is weaker than for the concessional outflows from multilateral core resources. As explored further in Box 4.7, this suggests that earmarking can be a way for donors to compensate for the lack of poverty focus in their direct bilateral engagements, possibly because they perceive their multilateral counterparts to have greater strengths in poverty reduction, be it their technical expertise in specific areas or their local presence.

## Figure 4.12. Multilateral organisations are able to focus on poverty through their concessional finance

Correlation coefficient between commitments in 2020-22 and poverty headcount of recipient countries

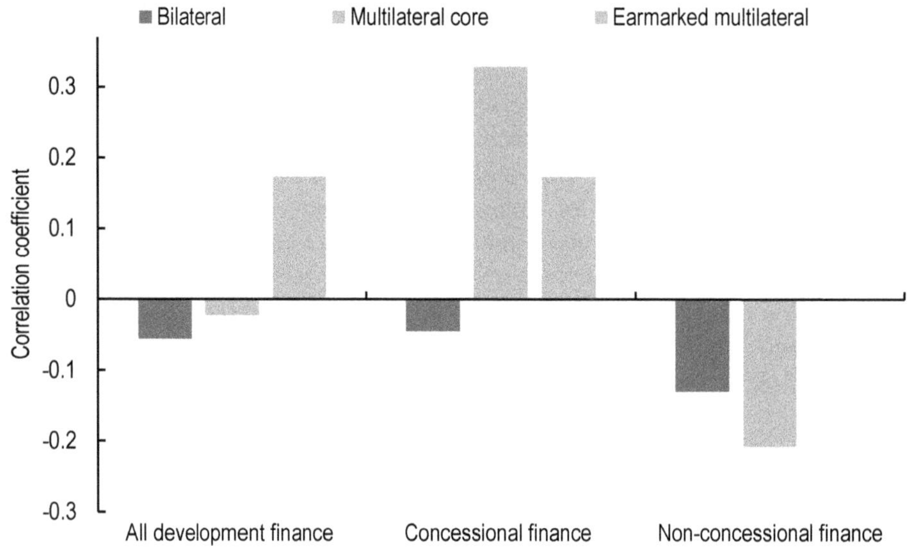


Note: Correlation coefficients between commitments and the most recent available poverty headcount ratio of developing countries, based on the World Bank's income poverty line of extreme poverty (USD 2.15/day). The data exclude finance allocated to regions and unspecified countries.

Source OECD (2024[1]), OECD Data Explorer, *Creditor Reporting System* (database), http://data-explorer.oecd.org/s/c., and World Bank (2023[14]), *World Development Indicators* (database), https://databank.worldbank.org/source/world-development-indicators.

**Multilateral providers' stronger poverty and inequality focus is also evident in their sectoral allocations.** Multilateral organisations tend to allocate greater portions of their development finance to social sectors than bilateral donors (Figure 4.13). An analysis of concessional and non-concessional finance between 2021 and 2022 reveals that social sectors were the top recipients of concessional outflows from multilateral organisations' core resources, accounting for 29% of the total (Figure 4.13, Panel A.). This share is higher than for purely bilateral (20%) and multilateral earmarked (25%) flows. For non-concessional finance, the production sector receives the largest shares of both multilateral and bilateral outflows, accounting for 39% and 55% respectively (Figure 4.13, Panel B). However, multilateral organisations still dedicate a sizable part (16%) of their non-concessional finance to social sectors, compared to only 1% for bilateral donors.

## Figure 4.13. Multilateral organisations prioritise social sectors more than bilateral donors

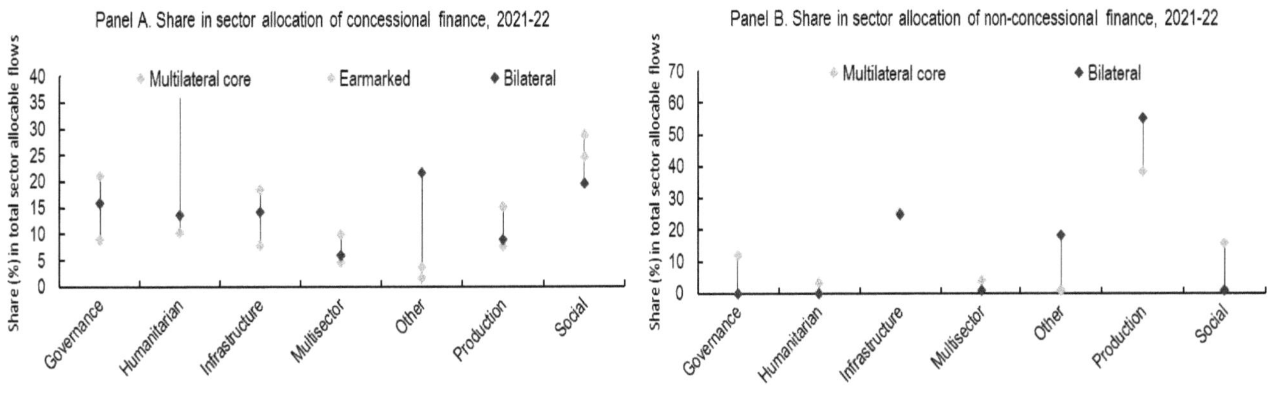


Note: Calculations are based on commitments, in 2022 constant prices.
Source: OECD (2024[1]), OECD Data Explorer, *Creditor Reporting System* (database), http://data-explorer.oecd.org/s/c.

### Box 4.7. How increasing earmarking for global public goods can reduce a focus on poverty

**Traditionally, earmarked funds channelled through the multilateral development system have displayed a relatively strong focus on the poorest countries.** Until 2020, the share of LDCs and other low-income countries in earmarked flows was consistently higher than that of core outflows (Figure 4.14). One possible reason for this tendency is that bilateral donors use earmarked contributions through multilateral organisations to ensure they are able to provide support in the most challenging contexts.

**Recently, however, donors appear to be moving away from an explicit poverty focus in their earmarking.** The share of LDCs and other LICs in earmarked flows decreased from 32% in 2020 to 25% in 2022, coinciding with a rise in flows not allocated to a particular country. It is likely that these unallocated flows relate to the provision of global public goods (GPGs) such as international pandemic preparedness and prevention, which target thematic or regional areas rather than individual countries. While these flows may eventually benefit LDCs and other LICs, they are not explicitly earmarked for the poorest countries.

**Figure 4.14. An increasing share of earmarked funds are unallocated, meaning less funds for low-income countries**

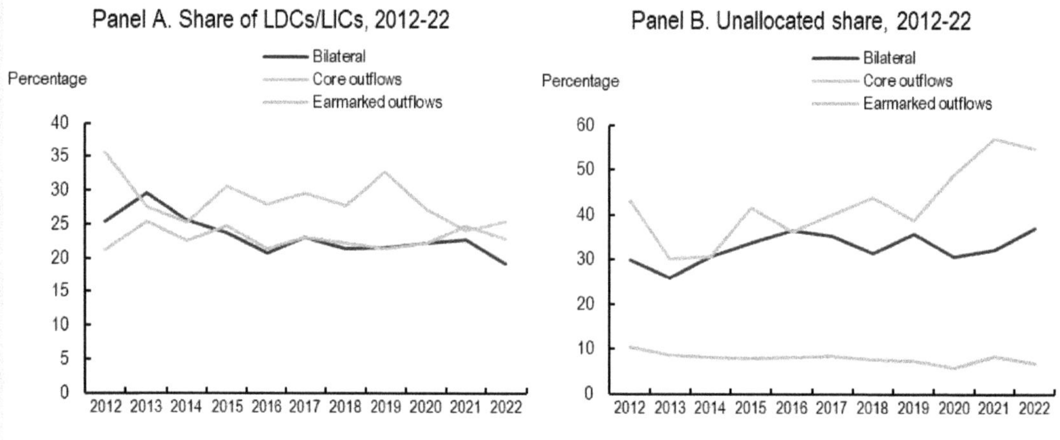


Note: Calculations are based on commitments, in 2022 constant prices.
Source: OECD (2024[1]), OECD Data Explorer, *Creditor Reporting System* (database), http://data-explorer.oecd.org/s/c.

**The share of earmarked funds that are related to global public goods is significantly higher in earmarked (35.6%) than in multilateral core outflows (10.4%)** (Figure 4.15), suggesting that bilateral donors use earmarking as a way to influence multilateral organisations to focus more on GPGs than they would do with their outflows from their core funds. Moreover, this tendency increased considerably in 2021, when the share of GPG-related earmarked flows rose to 40%, up from around 25-26% in previous years.

**Figure 4.15. Earmarked and core multilateral flows increasingly target global public goods**

Share of commitments targeting global public goods, 2012-22

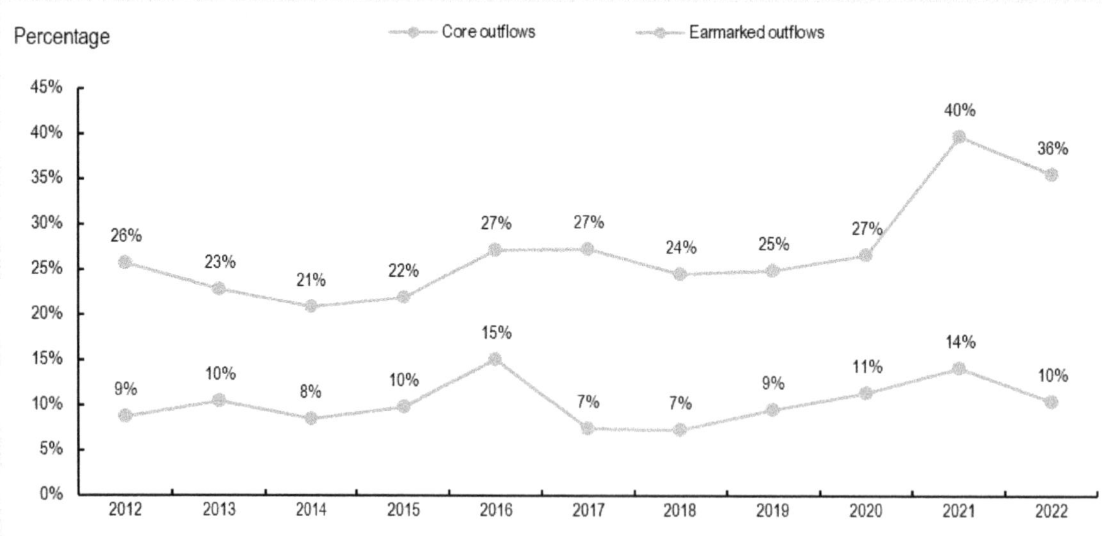


Note: Calculations are based on commitments, in 2022 constant prices.
Source: OECD (2024[1]), OECD Data Explorer, *Creditor Reporting System* (database), http://data-explorer.oecd.org/s/c.

**Beneath the overall patterns, there is considerable variation in the poverty focus among different types of organisations, reflecting their individual characteristics.** Of all the multilateral organisations, vertical funds show the strongest correlation between poverty in recipient countries and their commitment amounts (Figure 4.16). This is logical, as many of these funds, such as Gavi, largely provide concessional support and target the poorest and most vulnerable countries. Following them are UNDS entities, which also focus significantly on countries with the highest poverty headcount ratios. The World Bank Group also allocates more finance to countries with high levels of poverty as well as countries with higher inequality, in line with its twin goals of reducing poverty and fighting inequality.

### Figure 4.16. Different types of multilateral organisations vary in their poverty and inequality focus

Correlation between commitments in 2020-22 and Gini coefficient and poverty headcount ratio of recipient countries

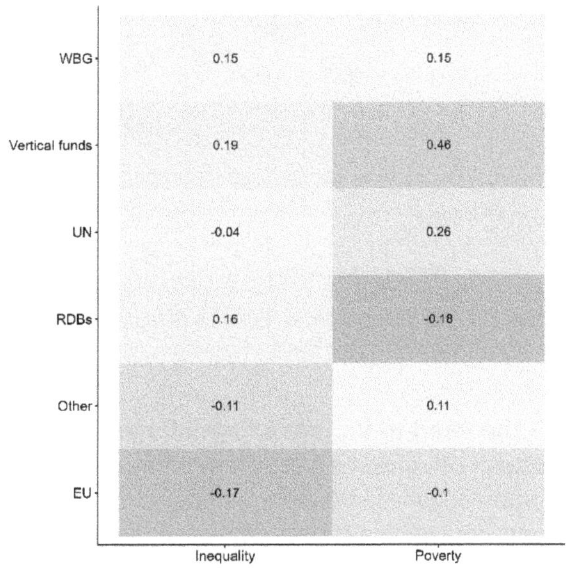


Note: Correlation coefficients between commitments and the most recent available income poverty headcount ratio and income inequality Gini index for developing countries
Source: OECD (2024[1]), OECD Data Explorer, *Creditor Reporting System* (database), http://data-explorer.oecd.org/s/c and World Bank (2023[14]), *World Development Indicators* (database), https://databank.worldbank.org/source/world-development-indicators.

## *Further intensifying leverage to scale up the system's financing capacity can compromise concessionality*

**There is a trade-off between the size and the concessionality of the finance provided by multilateral organisations.** Typically, organisations that exclusively provide concessional finance tend to commit fewer financial resources than those that provide both concessional and non-concessional finance. IDA is a notable exception in the multilateral development landscape, as it maintains a high share of concessional finance while being among the largest providers of finance among all multilateral entities.

**If not managed properly, this trade-off could end up limiting multilateral organisations' poverty focus.** Figure 4.17 traces the change in both the share of multilateral organisations' concessional finance and the overall volume of their financing between 2013-2015 and 2020-2022. It reveals that most organisations increased the size of their financial commitments over the period, some significantly. However, many of these organisations also reduced the proportion of concessional finance within their total commitments.

**Figure 4.17. Many multilateral organisations are increasing financing while reducing the share of concessional finance**

Change in outflows and change in share of concessional finance, 2013-15 versus 2020-22

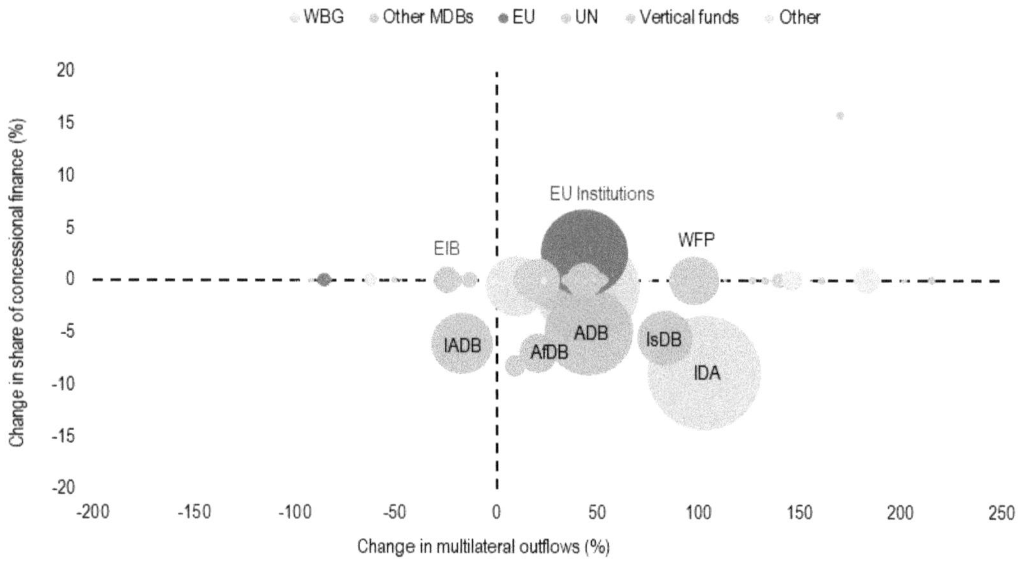


Note: Calculations are based on commitments, in 2022 constant prices. Bubble size represents volume of outflows.
Source: OECD (2024[1]), OECD Data Explorer, *Creditor Reporting System* (database), http://data-explorer.oecd.org/s/c.

**MDB reforms that emphasise the need to increase financial efficiency and better leverage balance sheets could limit the multilateral development system's capacity to address poverty.** While these reforms are enabling MDBs to substantially increase their financing, the increased reliance on leverage is likely to tilt the balance between concessional and non-concessional resources towards the latter. As discussed in Section 4.3.1, concessional and non-concessional finance vary significantly in their poverty focus. This tension between the pressure to scale up financing and the need to maintain concessionality may therefore affect the ability of multilateral organisations to target poverty effectively.

## Overview of key chapter findings and solutions

### *Key findings*

**The chapter highlights the significant trends and shifts in financing from the multilateral development system (multilateral outflows):**

- **The recovery of multilateral outflows in 2022 is a sign of the resilience and versatility of the multilateral development system amid multiple crises.** Multilateral organisations have demonstrated their ability to rebound quickly after the pandemic and swiftly adjust their sectoral allocations in response to evolving development needs. This resilience and adaptability constitutes one of the key strengths of the multilateral development system.
- **Multilateral organisations are leading the way in increasing private finance mobilisation and scaling up climate-related development finance**. In response to calls to revise their mandates to play a more prominent role in the provision of global public goods, multilateral organisations, and notably MDBs, have had considerable success in mobilising finance from private investors. At the same time, they have substantially scaled up climate-related development finance.

- **However, increasing pressures are revealing cracks in the multilateral development system that could undermine multilateral organisations' ability to address key development challenges.** Looking ahead, the poverty focus of multilateral development finance is at risk, as multilateral organisations are tasked with addressing a widening range of challenges and needs. The opportunities involved in the expansion of mandates can also become threats. Moreover, as ongoing reforms place greater expectations on the multilateral system, these organisations must balance long-term development goals – in particular poverty and inequality reduction – with the provision of global public goods and crisis response. Concentrating all efforts and resources on any one of these issues is already a significant challenge. Confronting all of them simultaneously could overstretch multilateral resources and lead to another trade-off between scaling up financing and maintaining concessionality. Ultimately, a shift towards less concessional resources will affect multilateral organisations' ability to target poverty and engage with countries facing public debt sustainability risks.

### *Key recommendations*

- **Safeguard the system's capacity to support the poorest and most vulnerable:** Preserve multilateral organisations' capacity to target poverty-relevant sectors and support the poorest and most vulnerable countries by monitoring the impact of their reforms and increasing their concessional resources.
    - Commission an assessment through the G20 or another relevant global forum to understand the impacts of recent and ongoing reforms on aid allocation across sectors, regions and country groupings.
    - Complement efforts to increase MDBs' financial leverage with measures to stock up their concessional resources, reversing the decade-long trend of stagnation in donor contributions.
- **Promote greater complementarity of multilateral aid portfolios:** Support research on multilateral aid portfolios at the sectoral and country levels, such as OECD portfolio similarity analyses, to inform multilateral reforms and programming. This can contribute to greater transparency, coherence and co-ordination among multilateral activities by clarifying their complementarity in terms of sector, geography and instrument.
- **Catalyse private investment:** Build on, and learn from, innovative portfolio approaches to tap into different sources of private finance, including institutional investors. Adopt clear criteria to evaluate the additionality and opportunity costs of blended finance initiatives, especially in least developed countries and other challenging contexts. Support a greater role for multilateral organisations in creating an environment conducive to private investment at the country level, such as by supporting initiatives to address risk misperceptions, to complement the current focus on deploying financial instruments at the project level.
- **Accelerate climate efforts in high-impact areas:** Ensure the additionality of multilateral climate finance and development finance, such as by targeting win-win investments to support country-led strategies. This includes strengthening efforts to expand adaptation finance, including by mainstreaming climate into sectors beyond infrastructure and production. Ensure climate diagnostics are embedded into country strategy and results frameworks. Improve and standardise climate reporting to rigorously assess the climate contribution of projects ex-ante and ex-post. Enhance co-ordination among multilateral and bilateral development partners through joint monitoring and knowledge work, including through country platforms.

## References


African Development Bank Group (2024), "African Development Bank Group Annual Meetings 2024: President Adesina calls for Bank makeover to attract game-changing private sector investment", https://www.afdb.org/en/news-and-events/press-releases/african-development-bank-group-annual-meetings-2024-president-adesina-calls-bank-makeover-attract-game-changing-private-sector-investment-71349. [15]

Bend, M. et al. (2023), *Education Finance Watch 2023*, World Bank Group, http://documents.worldbank.org/curated/en/099103123163755271/P17813506cd84f07a0b6be0c6ea576d59f8. [3]

Bhattacharya, A. et al. (2023), *A climate finance framework: decisive action to deliver on the Paris Agreement*, London School of Economics and Political Science, https://www.lse.ac.uk/granthaminstitute/publication/a-climate-finance-framework-decisive-action-to-deliver-on-the-paris-agreement-summary/. [11]

Convergence (2019), *Blending with Guarantees*, Convergence, https://www.convergence.finance/resource/blending-with-guarantees/view. [8]

COP28 (2023), "Multilateral development banks announce over $180 billion in new climate finance commitments through multi-year programs at COP28". [24]

Elgar, K. et al. (2023), *Development co-operation and the provision of global public goods*, OECD Publishing, Paris, https://doi.org/10.1787/aff8cba9-en. [27]

European Commission (2024), *European Fund for Sustainable Development Plus*, https://international-partnerships.ec.europa.eu/funding-and-technical-assistance/funding-instruments/european-fund-sustainable-development-plus_en. [13]

European Investment Bank (2023), *2022 Joint Report on Multilateral Development Banks' Climate Finance*, European Investment Bank, https://www.eib.org/en/publications/20230128-2022-joint-report-on-multilateral-development-banks-climate-finance (accessed on 4 June 2024). [25]

Farr, J., J. Morrissey and C. Donaldson (2022), *Unaccountable Accounting: The World Bank's unreliable climate finance reporting*, Oxfam International, https://policy-practice.oxfam.org/resources/unaccountable-accounting-the-world-banks-unreliable-climate-finance-reporting-621424/. [21]

G20 IEG (2023), *Strengthening Multilateral Development Banks: The Triple Agenda*, https://www.cgdev.org/sites/default/files/The_Triple_Agenda_G20-IEG_Report_Volume1_2023.pdf. [10]

Garbacz, W., D. Vilalta and L. Moller (2021), "The role of guarantees in blended finance", *OECD Development Co-operation Working Papers*, No. 97, OECD. [7]

Humphrey, C. and A. Prizzon (2014), *Guarantees for development A review of multilateral development bank operations*, ODI, https://odi.org/en/publications/guarantees-for-development-a-review-of-multilateral-development-bank-operations/. [9]

Lundsgaarde, E. (2023), *The future of EU blended finance and guarantees: an assessment of cooperation strategies with least developed countries in Africa*, IDOS, https://doi.org/10.23661/idp2.2023. [16]

Mathiasen, K., N. Lee and S. Matthews (2024), *IDA 21 and the Private Sector Window*, Center for Global Development, https://www.cgdev.org/publication/ida-21-and-private-sector-window. [17]

MDB Task Force on Mobilization (2024), *Mobilization of Private Finance by Multilateral Development Banks and Development Finance Institutions in 2022*, https://www.eib.org/attachments/press/mdb-joint-report-mobilization-of-private-finance-2022.pdf. [6]

Mitchell, I. and E. Wickstead (2024), *Has the $100 Billion Climate Goal Been Reached?*, Center for Global Development, https://www.cgdev.org/publication/has-100-billion-climate-goal-been-reached (accessed on 28 May 2024). [20]

MOPAN (2024), *Accelerating Climate Action: Multilateral Development Banks' Readiness and Performance, Lessons in Multilateral Effectiveness*, Multilateral Organisation Performance Assessment Network (MOPAN), https://www.mopanonline.org/analysis/items/MOPAN_LME_ClimateMDBS_.pdf. [26]

Núñez-Mujica, G., V. Ramachandran and S. Morris (2023), *What Counts as Climate? Preliminary Evidence from the World Bank's Climate Portfolio*, Center for Global Development, https://www.cgdev.org/publication/what-counts-climate-preliminary-evidence-world-banks-climate-portfolio. [22]

OECD (2024), "Climate-related development finance at the activity level: Recipient perspective (database), (accessed on 30 April, 2024)", *Dataset*, https://www.oecd.org/development/financing-sustainable-development/development-finance-topics/climate-change.htm. [18]

OECD (2024), *OECD Data Explorer, Creditor Reporting System (database), (accessed on 22 April, 2024)*, http://data-explorer.oecd.org/s/c. [1]

OECD (2024), *OECD Data Explorer, Mobilised private finance for development (database), (accessed on 30 April, 2024)*, http://data-explorer.oecd.org/s/q. [4]

OECD (2023), *Private finance mobilised by official development finance interventions*, OECD, Paris, https://www.oecd.org/en/publications/private-finance-mobilised-by-official-development-finance-interventions_c5fb4a6c-en.html. [5]

OECD (2022), *Multilateral Development Finance 2022*, OECD Publishing, Paris, https://doi.org/10.1787/9fea4cf2-en. [2]

OECD (forthcoming), *Biodiversity and Development Finance 2015-2022: Contributing to Target 19 of the Kunming-Montreal Global Biodiversity Framework*. [19]

UNFCCC Standing Committee on Finance (2021), *First Report on the Determination of the Needs of Developing Country Parties Related to Implementing the Convention and the Paris Agreement*, https://unfccc.int/sites/default/files/resource/54307_2%20-%20UNFCCC%20First%20NDR%20technical%20report%20-%20web%20%28004%29.pdf. [23]

World Bank (2023), "World Bank Group intensifies focus on private sector, launches effort to scale investment in emerging markets", *Press release*, https://www.worldbank.org/en/news/press-release/2023/06/22/world-bank-group-intensifies-focus-on-private-sector-launches-effort-to-scale-investment-in-emerging-markets. [14]

World Bank Group (2024), "World Bank Group prepares major overhaul to guarantee business", *Press release*, https://www.worldbank.org/en/news/press-release/2024/02/27/world-bank-group-prepares-major-overhaul-to-guarantee-business. [12]

## Notes

[1] Special purpose vehicles (SPV) are legal entities created to fulfil specific or temporary objectives. It can be used to isolate a company from financial risks of large investment projects, or to structure different layers of investment with different levels of risk participation in complex financing operations.

[2] Syndicated loans is a form of financing offered by a group of lenders, which allows lenders to take part in an investment loan, which is too large for them to extend on a standalone basis.

[3] Credit lines are extended to banks and other financial institutions, allowing continuous and repeated access to credit to flexibly respond to emergencies and evolving financing needs.

[4] Climate-related development finance is recorded differently for bilateral and multilateral donors:

All bilateral donors, and a few multilateral institutions, report their development activities that have climate objectives through the Rio markers. Data collection on ODA with Rio markers started in 1999 at the request of the UN conventions. Rio markers indicate if – and to what extent – a developmental activity has a principal or significant environmental objective.

MDBs – and most other multilateral institutions – report the climate component of their development finance activities, i.e. the share of their activities that is specifically devoted to climate action.

[5] Part of this rise is due to the fact that the number of reporting entities increased.

[6] The correlation coefficient between bilateral finance and poverty headcounts is negative and very low.

www.ingramcontent.com/pod-product-compliance
Ingram Content Group UK Ltd.
Pitfield, Milton Keynes, MK11 3LW, UK
UKHW051507290926
15471UKWH00008B/1468

9 789264 632035